RAISING A MENTALLY FIT GENERATION

RAISING A
MENTALLY FIT
GENERATION

Science-based tools and strategies to
build resilience and wellbeing in our kids

KARI SUTTON

Ask any parent what they want for their kids and they'll say something like … happiness and success; but what many really mean is that they want their children to be resilient and able to cope with life's ups and downs. In this book Kari draws on the research and presents practical advice for how parents can help their children foster and develop the crucial skills required for this; and she does it in a way that's easy to read and easy to apply.

Dr Timothy Sharp, Chief Happiness Officer – The Happiness Institute

Raising a Mentally Fit Generation is a practical, funny and scientifically researched guide for giving your children strong foundations for positive mental health and wellbeing. The easy-to-follow, evidence-backed recommendations are exactly what parents and teachers need today to support kids in their care to flourish. May this wonderful book reach all who need it.

Megan Dalla-Camina, Founder of Women Rising and best-selling author

Kari's extensive knowledge and experience in applying positive psychology and mental fitness practices has made a significant impact in the education sector over many years. There are very few programs and books showing educators and parents how to build positive mental health activities that can be easily incorporated into the everyday life of children to build habits to support their wellbeing during the good times and the bad. This book is a "must read" for anyone working with young children, especially those with significant challenges.

Paula Robinson, PhD, Executive Director and CEO
Applied Positive Psychology Learning Institute

Raising a Mentally Fit Generation provides parents with practical advice that is both accessible and transformative. It's filled with real-life stories and science-based, practical advice. Read it, read it again, and then more importantly, apply it.

Judeth Wilson, Director of WeTrain and The Trainers Ultimate Toolkit and Ever-Learning Mum

I loved this book. It is a fabulous read, so easy to digest with some great tips and tricks along the way. The book is supported by robust science and Kari's unique experience in this field. This is a must read and will add tremendously to the conversation about mental health and wellbeing, about raising mentally fit children, and being the best parent we can be. Well done Kari on a wonderful achievement.

Sue Langley, CEO Langley Group

Raising a Mentally Fit Generation is the book we all need right now. It is engaging and practical – setting out a clear path for parents, early childhood educators and teachers, enabling them to help lay foundations in our young people so they can thrive in this changing world. Both conversational and compelling, it delivers vital tools and approaches for equipping children with the skills and habits they will need to be mentally and emotionally fit for their bright futures.

Justine Peacock, Coach & Psychotherapist and parent

No parent expects to be perfect, yet my greatest fear is failing to provide my daughter with the wellbeing tools she needs to grow and develop. In a world of media noise and peer pressure from other parents, *Raising a Mentally Fit Generation* is the breath of fresh air every parent needs to support their little ones. It's our go-to practical guide for the realities modern children face, and for issues classic parenting books don't cover. My wife and I knew what to expect when we were expecting; we are now empowered to raise a positive, resilient child ready for whatever the future holds.

Jacob Aldridge, Host of the *Come Again?* IVF Podcast

The perfect combination of theory and practice! What every parent needs – no judgment, practical ideas, and a way forward. *Raising a Mentally Fit Generation* will be relevant twenty years from now as it captures how to equip our young people with the skills they need to be emotionally fit now and in the future. An outstanding read!

Roxanne Smith, Deputy Principal, and mum of
two beautiful girls

Raising a mentally fit generation is everyone's responsibility. We need to do things differently and help young people become and stay mentally fit. This work gives us tools to help young people build mental fitness muscles and develop seven key habits. Kari has distilled the science into ten components and brought this to you in a very readable and memorable way. Parents, schools and young people need to read this, discuss it and share it.

Professor Lindsay G. Oades, Director Centre for Positive Psychology, The University of Melbourne

First published in 2020 by Kari Sutton

© 2020 Kari Sutton

The moral rights of the author have been asserted

A catalogue entry for this book is available from the National Library of Australia.

ISBN: 978-1-922391-33-9

Project management and text design by Publish Central
Cover design by Peter Reardon

Disclaimer

The material in this publication is of the nature of general comment only, and does not represent professional advice. It is not intended to provide specific guidance for particular circumstances and it should not be relied on as the basis for any decision to take action or not take action on any matter which it covers. Readers should obtain professional advice where appropriate, before making any such decision. To the maximum extent permitted by law, the author and publisher disclaim all responsibility and liability to any person, arising directly or indirectly from any person taking or not taking action based on the information in this publication.

Contents

Dedication

To Andrew, I treasure our love and life together. To Mitchell, who fills my life with joy.

To my parents Anne and Jerry and brother Mark for their encouragement, love and support.

This work is also dedicated to all the children and families at Camp Quality who left imprints on my heart that will stay with me forever. Thank you for teaching me that we can all be equipped with a toolkit of attitudes, behaviours and strategies that promote positive mental health and wellbeing, no matter what our life circumstances.

A note from the author

As I was finishing this book, Australia was being ravaged by bushfires and was in the grip of one of the worst bushfire seasons we have ever had. Families, children, communities and wildlife were all hurting. I received numerous calls and emails from parents worried about how their children would bounce back from this unfathomable disaster. Our capacity to bounce back from crises, to be resilient, is moulded throughout childhood. Just like we can put actions in place to prepare our families and homes for fires, we can prepare our kids for the firestorms of life.

For the past two decades, I've had the privilege of helping raise my nephew Mitchell after my beloved sister-in-law passed away from ovarian cancer. I was presented with this opportunity when my brother reached out for support after they had been through their own personal firestorm. As a family, we've experienced many of the same problems and concerns raising him as every other parent has, and I have always appreciated the support and chance to talk these things through with other parents. I used the tools and strategies I learned through my positive psychology studies to begin building his mental fitness muscles so that he would be able to tackle anything else life threw his way. I have also tested these ideas with thousands of other children and families, which brought me to my work today and the book you're reading right now.

When clients and colleagues approached me to write this book my first thought was – who am I to write a book? I am not a psychiatrist, I am not a psychologist, and I don't have a PhD. Then one of the mums I had the pleasure of working with put it to me this way.

She said, "Kari, I got a lot out of the stories, ideas and tools you shared. I know they helped my family and I believe they could help others. Isn't that worth it?"

Throughout my career, I have always wanted to be of service to others and help children and their families in any way I can. That's why I became a teacher, then a guidance counsellor and spent over 22 years volunteering with Camp Quality, a children's cancer charity. This book is the combination of my research and my everyday experiences as part-time parent for my nephew, a volunteer at Camp Quality, a teacher and guidance counsellor with over 25 years of experience in the education system. I am determined to change the conversation about how we promote good mental health in children as well as empower people who care for, and work with, children (parents, grandparents, carers, early childhood educators, teachers) to plant the seeds of resilience, emotional wellbeing and mental fitness.

I know that a proactive preventative approach is crucial. As parents, we want to prevent problems occurring by building strong protective fences at the top of the cliff rather than waiting to be the ambulances at the bottom, picking our children up when things have gone wrong. Talking to children about their mental fitness from a young age can help them become more resilient and teach them how to look after themselves mentally as well as physically.

It's essential for me that the information and ideas presented in this book are relevant, detailed and well-researched but it is just a guide. What is best for you and your children will depend on your personal circumstances. For this reason, if you do require more information, guidance or support concerning any particular issue I would ask that you please speak with your medical practitioner, counsellor or mental health practitioner who will be able to take the time to understand your family's individual circumstances and needs.

Thank you for taking the time to read this book. I hope you find it a useful tool that helps us, and our world, raise a mentally fit generation of kids.

With deepest gratitude,

Kari Sutton

Introduction

As a parent, it's scary to realise that your child's adult brain and coping ability is pretty much set by age seven, so you've got to put in the hard yards early on.

Alice Williams

Imagine you are walking your child up to their classroom to drop them off to school. You put their bag in the racks outside their classroom and hug them goodbye, hoping your precious baby won't worry so much that they end up feeling sick the entire day.

You're standing there staring through the window at your child's class of 28 beautiful children, wondering how on earth you're going to help your child through the debilitating anxiety that they come home with every afternoon.

As those 28 buzzing children go to take their seats ready to begin their day, you may not be aware that out of those 28 children:

* one has been diagnosed with depression
* two have hurt themselves in times of extreme stress and anxiety

★ seven are experiencing ongoing mental health conditions – losing sleep because of worry and anxiety

★ many others in the room are the victims, or perpetrators, of bullying.

> This is modern childhood, and as adults who care for the children in our lives, we must ask ourselves – what has gone so wrong?

Why adults are understandably worried

The nature of children's health around the world is changing. There is now a 'new morbidity' occurring, with obesity, mental health conditions, self-harm and suicide taking centre stage. Having worked as a teacher and guidance counsellor for the past 25 years, I have had a front-row seat watching the dramatic rise in anxiety disorders, depression and suicide affecting our kids.

According to the Australian Bureau of Statistics, over 560,000 Australian children and young people have mental health problems and the World Health Organization's report into child and adolescent mental health illustrates that these statistics are reflected in the USA, Canada, the United Kingdom and Europe. If left untreated, these conditions severely influence children's development, their educational attainments and their potential to live fulfilling and productive lives.

What this means for us as parents is that our children are now part of the following statistics:

* 1 in 4 young Australians have a mental health condition

* 1 in 4 Australian primary school students are losing sleep through worry and anxiety

* 1 in 5 Australian primary school students surveyed have been bullied three-plus times at school in the last 12 months

* In Australia, the presentation of both boys and girls with mental health problems to psychologists and psychiatrists has tripled over the past 10 years

* In the UK, a 2017 report by the Children's Commissioner found that 800,000 young people – equivalent to the population of the city of Manchester – suffer from mental health conditions

* There has been a 10 per cent increase in the number of deaths through suicide among children between five and 17 since 2016. Suicide remains the leading cause of death in this age group, with 98 deaths in 2017 within Australia

* A 2019 study investigating the United States emergency room data from 2007 to 2015 found that annual visits for suicidal thoughts and suicide attempts among children age 5 to 18 nearly doubled – from 580,000 to 1.12 million.

These statistics are not merely numbers on a page; they are young people who each have a name, a face, a family and a future.

Parents today are feeling overwhelmed and don't know what to do

A poll by the Victorian Royal Children's Hospital in 2017 found that only a third of parents are confident they could recognise the signs of a mental health problem in their child.

A report from the Australian Childhood Foundation found that 56 per cent of parents lack confidence in their parenting, which is not that much of a surprise as there isn't a manual that teaches us how to parent. I recognise I haven't been perfect in my parenting practices over the years (you'll learn about the mistakes I made and things I wish I had done differently throughout *Raising a Mentally Fit Generation*) and know that many of my friends feel the same way. We can always strive to do better, and that begins by gaining more knowledge about what works.

Life is a lot more uncertain than when we were growing up and this presents countless social, emotional, physical and mental health challenges for both parents and kids. Many of us are just surviving and are unsure about the best ways to develop our children's mental fitness muscles so that they can grow into resilient, happy adolescents and adults.

In early 2009 I began running workshops for parents, teachers, schools and early childhood services focusing on how those adults can help children in their care to thrive, not just survive. These workshops seemed to strike a chord – the adults who came were worried about their children and were eager for any guidance I could give them. When I asked people what they wanted most for the children in their lives, they universally identified that they wanted their kids to be happy, to handle the issues and challenges of day-to-day life and bounce back from adversity. Every parent I have ever worked with has had similar goals – to help their kids develop into well-adjusted, kind, resilient young people who have a zest for life.

The good news is as significant adults for our children, the real difference is in our hands; the parenting practices we use have a substantial influence on our children's psychological wellbeing. Almost 50 per cent of the factors that determine children's psychological wellbeing and happiness come from the environments in which they are raised. This doesn't mean that genetics don't play a part. But as Daniel Goleman, an expert in emotional and social intelligence, describes in his book *Social Intelligence*, 'it is biologically impossible for a gene to operate independently of its environment, genes are designed to be regulated by signals from their immediate surroundings.' This means that there is a lot we can do to ensure our children reach their own unique potential and develop their own healthy, strong psychological wellbeing that enables them to face the future with confidence.

This book is about how every adult who comes into contact with children can foster the mindsets, habits, tools and skills that children need for psychological wellbeing throughout childhood, adolescence and into adult life.

Why this book and why now

Everything in this book has been drawn from research related to psychological wellbeing. It takes key findings from the new field of positive psychology and combines them with valuable knowledge from developmental cognitive neuroscience and emotional intelligence, to provide evidence-based strategies and ideas about how both parents and children can develop psychological wellbeing and begin to thrive.

The last two decades have witnessed increasing empirical research that has provided us with rich data about what people need to thrive and fulfil their potential. As a researcher and educator, I have made it my goal to follow the emerging research and translate it into simple, practical strategies and tools that parents I work with can immediately implement in their day-to-day lives to sow the seeds of psychological wellbeing in their children and help them develop habits that will last a lifetime.

I was fortunate to study with Martin Seligman in 2003 and 2004 exploring the emerging science of human flourishing and how this research could provide practical ways for parents, grandparents, extended family members, teachers, early childhood professionals, coaches and other significant adults in children's lives to help children build the skills and mindsets they need to thrive. I translated the research into practical applications that I have used in my work with over 25,000 children, parents, teachers and early childhood educators throughout Australia. Our kids are intelligent and can use the information we give them to shape the architecture of their brain and the way it functions and responds to different situations.

It's up to us to provide them with the knowledge and tools they need to become the best versions of themselves.

Good enough really is good enough

One key point I do want to stress is that as parents, we haven't broken our kids. The absolute majority of parents that I have worked with over the past 25 years have been doing the best they can and have the best interests of their children at heart.

As parents, we have all experienced feeling guilty, possibly on a regular basis. This can make us feel that even when we are trying our best, it's not good enough and there is so much more we could, and should, be doing for our kids to make sure they are happy, healthy and well-adjusted.

One mum I worked with explained it this way. "Since having my kids, I haven't stopped feeling guilty. I worry that I haven't given them the best start in life because I haven't done things the 'right' way and I don't get stuff perfect."

None of us are perfect and good enough really is good enough – sometimes baked beans are all that we can muster, and that is okay. It's our patterns and habitual ways of doing things that matter most – not the one-off occasions when things go a little pear-shaped.

Perfect parents and perfect kids don't exist anywhere except on other people's social media feeds of course, and yet we all keep judging ourselves harshly if we don't live up to our own expectations. Acknowledging that we all have our good and not so good days and that we are trying to raise our kids in the best ways we can and have their best interests at heart is a significant part of taking care of our own psychological well-being. Raising children is a lesson in flexibility and tolerance, learning to roll with the waves that come and give ourselves the kindness we deserve on *those* days. We all have bad days and that doesn't make us bad parents. Expecting perfection from our children, or ourselves, sets us up for frustration, disappointment, stress and anxiety, all of which are detrimental to both our own and our kids' mental fitness.

It's important to remember that there is no one right way to do something, especially parenting, and that having perfection as a standard is the best way to set yourself up to fail.

Stop comparing yourself to other people on social media as these images are carefully curated and provide only the version people want you to see – not what is truly happening in their lives.

Every day we have opportunities to help our kids build their mental fitness muscles and resilience.

> We can help them develop habitual behaviours and ways of thinking that become encoded ways of automatically thinking and responding.

We successfully did this with the 'slip, slop slap' campaign, and the rates of skin cancer plummeted because both adults and kids became used to those habits and now don't go out in the sun without their hats, sunscreen and long-sleeved shirts.

Now it's time to turn our attention inwards to their mental wellbeing and habits. We need to help our kids develop daily habits that take care of their mental health – just like they take care of their physical health by exercising and eating enough fruit and vegetables. These habits need to become second nature, just like putting on their sunscreen so that we can prevent mental health problems such as anxiety, depression, self-harm and suicide occurring.

I'd like you to again imagine that you are walking your child up to their classroom. They know exactly where to place their bag, they call out to a few friends and then say goodbye to you without any tears. When you see them again at the end of the day, they chat happily about their day and talk about strategies they used to deal with different situations they faced.

This is how we raise a mentally fit generation.

Ready?

How to use this book

Our lives are led at such a fast pace it can be a challenge to find the time to sit and read. I have designed the book so you can dip in and out of it whenever you have the time. You'll gain the most benefit if you could read it start to finish. However, if you are finding that challenging, dip straight into the areas you find most interesting. The book has been designed as a smorgasbord menu, not a prescription, so dive into the activities and give them a try. Most of the ideas don't cost a lot of money or take a considerable amount of time. You can pick and choose what works for you and your children – different things will work for different people, and your children may like activities that you're not that keen on. That's okay – all of them will develop your child's mental fitness.

In the first chapter, I unpack the concept of mental fitness, why it matters, and most importantly, what you can do to develop both your own mental fitness and that of your children. I then briefly outline research from the field of positive psychology about the key building blocks of mental fitness. People with high levels of psychological wellbeing are happier, more successful, have more and better relationships, are physically healthier, do better academically, and are more resilient, which are all things that we want for our children.

The following ten chapters each focus on an important component of mental fitness and positive mental health. Each chapter provides a brief summary of the research behind the component, how, and why, it contributes to mental fitness and positive mental health, as well as a variety of practical activities and ideas to try contained in a GET FIT NOW section. There are also three questions at the end of each chapter that will encourage you to think about the ideas and how you could apply them in your life to foster your child's wellbeing.

Any one component will help build your child's mental fitness, and the more you can implement, the better. Even small actions can build both happy families and resilient kids. You don't have to get everything right – simply develop these skills and mindsets as best you can, and your children will thrive.

The purpose of this book is to examine ways we can cultivate children's mental fitness in the early childhood years. However, the book is relevant for every parent, as people of all ages benefit from developing positive habits of mind. It is never too early or too late to build your mental fitness.

I have filled the pages with practical tried-and-tested information and ideas as well as stories that have been drawn from my work with over 25,000 children, parents, teachers and early childhood educators (all stories are true, only the names have been changed).

The adults I work with are extremely worried about the levels of anxiety, depression and self-harm their children and young people are experiencing. The more time I spend with parents and educators, the more I have come to understand their lack of confidence tackling the complicated issues impacting their children's mental health and wellbeing. I have written this book as a guide to provide both parents and other significant adults in children's lives with the knowledge, strategies and resources to help their children develop mental fitness which acts as a protective and preventative factor against mental ill-health.

> The way we raise our children has a ripple effect on society – it influences the type of adults they become, how they parent their children, and then how those children parent their children.

I have no doubt we can raise a mentally fit generation of strong, resilient, compassionate and kind human beings.

The protective nature
of mental fitness

Up until the mid-1970s, health promotion activities were virtually non-existent. Governments around the world had focused mainly on reactive measures that stressed the early detection of illness followed by potent treatment. During the early 1970s, the emphasis changed to health-promoting activities and behaviours rather than simply waiting to treat a disease when it occurred. There was a big focus on physical fitness as it was recognised that it could improve people's health and reduce the risks of developing lifestyle-based diseases. Public health authorities around the world, along with the World Health Organization, have agreed that the majority of diseases in the 20th century are caused by lifestyle factors, meaning that the choices we make and actions we take can either erode or support our health and wellbeing.

In society today, physical fitness gets a lot of attention; we know that being physically fit can prevent certain conditions like heart disease and diabetes. We also know that to be physically fit, you need to participate in activities regularly as fitness cannot be stored, so we have to work at developing habits that help us maintain or improve our physical fitness.

Imagine if I asked you, "How's your child's physical fitness?" You'd most probably be able to answer that fairly quickly. You would know how strong or flexible they are as well as their ability to endure physical exertion. Being physically fit is better than simply being healthy – it's functioning at an optimal level with better flexibility and strength as well as good endurance. But if I asked you, "How's your child's mental fitness?" you may not be able to answer as readily.

What is mental fitness?

Dr Paula Robinson, who has studied mental fitness over the past 15 years, defines it as 'learning skills and ways to build our ability to meet challenges successfully and thrive in our environment.' Mental fitness is not 'thinking positively' all the time or training our brains with puzzles and quizzes. It's about possessing the needed mindsets, skills, abilities and experience to cope with situations and challenges as they happen.

The mental fitness model, outlined in Dr Robinson's book, *Practising Positive Education: A guide to improving wellbeing literacy in schools*, is a proactive approach to developing positive mental health. It focuses on strength, endurance, flexibility and the concept of team. Each of the components covered in the following chapters contributes to one of the core concepts of strength, endurance, flexibility and team, and by implementing the suggested activities regularly, you can help your children develop positive habits of mind.

A common misunderstanding is that people with a high level of mental fitness are continually optimistic and do not experience negative emotions or thoughts. This is not the case; mentally fit people have simply built habits, mindsets and strategies into their lives that help them to effectively navigate challenges with relative ease.

> Mental fitness is a precursor to resilience, and the best way to support our children and young people in developing positive mental health and wellbeing is to teach them the protective skills and tools they need to deal with challenges before they need them.

It seems extraordinary to need to talk about how we can promote good mental health in our children. Childhood is supposed to be an untroubled time in life, free from the stresses and burdens of adulthood and pressures of the modern world. As parents, we often assume that our kids innately have good mental health habits that will help prepare them for handling life's inevitable challenges.

Regrettably, this is not the case. According to the Australian Bureau of Statistics, over 14 per cent of children and young people have mental health problems, and 50 per cent of adult mental health disorders originate before the age of 14. The World Health Organization has found that these statistics are also reflected in the USA, Canada, the United Kingdom and Europe. Research from the Children's Commissioner in the

UK has shown that parents are more likely to seek services when symptoms become severe or impact significantly on the child's ability to function.

If mental health problems are not proactively addressed, they become more established and harder to remedy. Then they will have enduring implications such as increased risk of mental health disorders in adulthood, poor educational achievement, possible unemployment, contact with the criminal justice system and poorer health outcomes.

> Having good mental fitness and positive mental health does not preclude kids from experiencing problems or obstacles. Feeling sad, worried, fearful or anxious when trying new things is normal. Kids who are mentally fit are prepared to handle the challenges that come their way.

Benefits of mental fitness

The question 'Do kids need to be mentally fit?' is rarely asked until a crisis occurs.

As a teacher and guidance counsellor, I witnessed hundreds of kids develop significant mental health problems because they didn't have the skills, mindsets and tools they needed to deal with challenges, setbacks, failure and rejection.

My two decades of volunteering with Camp Quality, a children's cancer charity that supports children aged up to 13 coping with the daily ups and downs of dealing with cancer, provided me with a profound realisation; we can all be equipped with a toolkit of attitudes, behaviours and strategies that promote good mental health and wellbeing no matter what our life circumstances.

The kids at Camp Quality challenged my thinking both as a teacher and guidance officer. I worked with children and young people who were struggling with wellbeing yet hadn't experienced anywhere near the same obstacles the campers at Camp Quality had lived through. I would walk back into school, look through my classroom window at these children, and wonder why we couldn't get it right for them.

Being mentally fit can help prevent mental health conditions such as anxiety and depression from occurring. Mentally fit kids feel better in themselves, are more creative and can deal with stressful situations such as bullying or exams more calmly and with less anxiety.

Helping children build their mental fitness muscles provides them with the skills they need to deal with hardships, failure, setbacks and rejection. Just like we can help children develop their physical fitness, we can also help them develop the attitudes, mindsets and habits that build their mental fitness muscles.

As with physical fitness, mental fitness cannot be stored, so we need to help our children proactively employ regular, intentional activities that form positive habits of mind.

The earlier we start teaching our kids these skills, the better equipped they'll be for the realities of adolescence and adulthood.

Building our mental fitness muscles

Most of us have not been taught mental fitness skills and positive habits of mind by our families or at school. Some people will be naturally 'fitter' than others, but the good news is that we can all develop the skills and tools we need to improve our mental strength, endurance and flexibility.

Parents' capability to cultivate mental fitness in our children is greatly contingent on our own mental fitness. The ways in which we nurture and develop our own mental fitness serve as a template for our children. By modelling good mental fitness habits, tools and strategies that take care of ourselves and our psychological wellbeing, we are embedding protective factors that lessen the probability of developing anxiety, depression and other mental health difficulties. In exactly the same way airline staff instruct us to put our own oxygen masks on first before helping others, we need to make sure we take care of ourselves first as we can't take care of anyone else if we are running on empty. Our children soak in every action we take, and when they see us caring for ourselves by eating well, exercising, making time for friends, laughing and having fun, using our strengths and taking some time out to rest, they notice that these things help us function better.

Sometimes you're hit by challenges; things can become too much and overwhelm us. If this does happen, please make sure you ask for help. It's not a sign of weakness; in fact, it's a sign of strength. It demonstrates that you're self-aware enough to know that you need support and help to work through it all. Being honest and open about this helps our kids understand that there's nothing wrong with asking for help or seeking support when things have gone awry. In 2009 I developed adrenal fatigue and knew that I needed to go and see someone to help with the underlying causes. I spoke with Mitchell and my husband about this to ensure that Mitchell understood that seeking help from a psychologist or other mental health professional is a natural thing to do and does not have any stigma attached.

Raising kids can, at times, feel very isolating and lonely, even in our hyperconnected world.

So many mums that I have worked with throughout the past two and a half decades have confided in me that they're often lonely and feel disconnected from the world they occupied before they had kids. We need to make sure that we assemble a village both for ourselves and our kids. A strong network of other parents, trusted friends, grandparents, extended family and neighbours provides our kids with a profound sense of security and helps make raising children feel much less isolating and lonely.

I know from personal experience that having someone to talk to and confide in helped me feel safe and supported when I was wondering if the way I was raising Mitchell was the right thing to do for a child whose mother had died at such a young age. It also opened the doors for others to share their experiences with me, which built connections and friendships that last to this day. When Mitchell was little, it was mainly through playgroups, his kindergarten, and my church that I assembled our village. Today I see plenty of villages being formed online through social media, especially with the families I work with who live in regional or remote areas whose extended families are a long way away. Whatever way works for you; find a network, group or tribe where you feel you fit, and I am sure you will make a difference in other parents' lives by being there.

Becoming mentally fit takes commitment and practice, which might sound like a lot of work. But the effort we devote to embedding these skills, routines and tools into our daily lives pays off handsomely, setting our children up for success both at school and in life. One mum explained her experience like this – "It took some serious effort and focus from my husband and me, but we've been able to help the twins develop more of a growth mindset. We've modelled growth mindset thinking with phrases like, 'what am I missing?', 'we can always improve' and 'mistakes help us learn'. They even catch me out sometimes when I say I don't know how to do something, saying, 'Mum, you don't know how to do it yet'". These parents worked hard to habitually embed the language and ideas of a growth mindset into their everyday lives so that their twins would grow up being okay making mistakes, learning from failures and be able to tackle hard things head-on. It wasn't always easy for them and they had to be open to new ways of thinking and different ways of raising their children, which didn't come automatically. I work with many parents who are keen to learn new concepts and skills, which weren't passed on to them when they were growing up. They know these are important tools for their kids' mental health and understand that they need to apply the concepts and skills in their own lives so that they can set good examples for their children.

Mental fitness on autopilot

When I was teaching, I wanted my preschool and kindergarten classes to run like well-oiled machines where the children automatically put their lunch boxes away in the basket, their bags in their cubbyholes and put the books away before getting the blocks out. To make this happen, I had to put in some serious time and work developing class routines that eventually turned into habits the children would automatically do. Sometimes at the beginning of the year working with three and four-year-olds, it felt like it was going to take forever, but the results were worth the effort.

Just like I taught the students in my classes the skills to orga-
nise and tidy up after themselves, mental fitness is a skill set
that we can teach our kids.

> We need to start educating our children about the importance
> of mental wellbeing – just like we do with exercise, healthy eat-
> ing and wearing sunscreen.

Over time our daily habitual behaviours and thoughts create
who we are. As parents and other significant adults in children's lives, it's our responsibility to help our children develop
positive, healthy habits of mind that foster resilience and
wellbeing so they can flourish and thrive.

The building blocks of mental fitness

Being a parent is a complex and challenging role with many
different priorities competing for your time. Each of us will
have different ideas about how to raise a happy, resilient child.
There are, however, some essential building blocks you can
put into place to help your child develop their mental fitness
muscles. Think of it in a similar way to building a house; you
need to ensure there are strong foundations before you begin
building your dream home, otherwise you may find yourself
with real problems moving forward. That's why I encourage
parents to involve their kids in regular, intentional activities that form positive habits of mind every day. This will

strengthen the neural connections that form the foundations for a child's resilience and wellbeing.

> Any of our actions or ways of thinking will become habitual patterns if we repeat them frequently enough. These pathways become set in our brains and are then the automatic ways we respond.

A good example of this is learning to drive. I know my first few lessons were a nightmare for both my parents and I, until I'd practised enough that the skill of driving had become almost second nature as the patterns were hardwired into my brain. I have repeated those patterns so often that I can now drive listening to music, thinking about my day, and I don't even remember the actual driving process because I am operating on autopilot. David Neal, an Executive in Residence at Duke University, found that this is what happens with our emotions and behaviours as well.

Once our emotions, behaviours and actions become our automatic ways of responding, they run permanently in the background, like an operating system on your computer. They become unconscious habits of mind that control almost everything that happens in our lives, and we're not even aware they are running in the background. The following seven actions are intentional behaviours that can be established as habits within your family and provide a solid foundation for your child's good mental health and wellbeing.

Seven habits for mental fitness

1. Have a clear direction

As a family discuss what values are important in your lives – what does your family stand for? This helps children understand what is right and wrong and guides them in knowing what they need to do in different situations. My husband, Mitchell and I used to have these conversations around the dinner table together, which helped Mitch understand how to behave in different situations he found himself in at school and socially.

2. Be a positive role model

You are your child's first and most important teacher. Parents are the primary role-models children see, and therefore our primary teaching device is the example we set. If they see us exercising every day, they will come to see that as a normal part of life. If they observe us worrying and hear us focusing on the negative side of things and what can go wrong, that will become part of their repertoire of how to handle things. After Mitchell's mum died, I was very conscious of the role models he had around him, and that is why I stepped in to help parent him because my brother was falling apart and was not the best role model for Mitchell at that time.

3. Develop routines

Regardless of your parenting style, one of the most important things you can do is to establish as much routine in your children's lives as possible. Routines help children feel safe and secure, predict what is coming next and learn what is expected of them. This does not mean you can't be flexible and spontaneous at different times but that you are consistent with what you expect. You can also develop routines for how you deal with negative thoughts, think more optimistically or relax at the end of the day.

4. Set clear, consistent boundaries

Clear boundaries and rules that are applied consistently help children learn what is expected of them. Ensure the boundaries and rules are clear, easy to understand and framed in a positive way. Remind your children of your expectations and consistently enforce them. Kids will push back on boundaries when you are starting to implement them, and this is okay. It can take quite a while before a child willingly accepts a parent's boundaries. You can tell when this is occurring because they start to cry, scream and push back less than they did at the beginning.

5. Sleep

Sleep is vital for healthy brain development. It helps us deal with, and learn from, events of the day. Kids and teenagers' brains are regularly cultivating new neural connections. They absolutely must have enough sleep to nurture these connections. One of the most basic things you can do for your kids' health, wellbeing and behaviour is to make sure they get the sleep they need. Establishing healthy sleep habits and routines is a critical building block not only for their mental fitness but also for their physical health.

6. Communicate

It is vital that you and your children develop good communication habits. If this occurs from a young age, you will be more likely to continue this as they grow. Really try and be present when you are talking with your child as they will be able to tell if your mind is somewhere else. Actively listen – pay close attention to what your child is saying and then paraphrase what they said and how they are feeling to check if you have it right. This way, they will know you are listening and want to understand. When praising children use specific descriptive praise to let them know exactly what it is you have appreciated. For example, "Jamie, I like the way you picked your clothes up off the floor." This sense of recognition fosters children's feelings of being valued by others.

7. Spend time being present

Due to our hectic lifestyles and other pressures, it can be difficult for families to spend time together on a regular basis. I know that I have often felt like there were so many other things that needed to be done instead of simply spending time with Mitchell. However, I knew it was vitally important to spend both quality time and a good quantity of time with him to help him develop into the young man I knew he could be. I, therefore, made a conscious effort to be present and focus on what I was doing with him, to enjoy the moment. I knew other things could wait, and they would still be there when we finished.

As children grow up, they won't remember the things they were given – yes, those are lovely, but the majority won't stick in their memories for that long. Instead, they will remember meaningful experiences they've had with you, extended family or their friends. Frequently these activities have minimal cost – things like throwing a frisbee around and having a picnic in the park, blowing bubbles at the beach, kicking a football. They all have one thing in common: you do them together. That's what kids really want – quality time spent with you.

> Habits are hard to break. The earlier in life we can help our children develop positive habits of mind that increase their mental fitness, the easier it is for them to keep these going throughout their lives into adolescence and adulthood.

IN A NUTSHELL

★ Being mentally fit can help prevent mental health conditions such as anxiety and depression from occurring.

★ Mental fitness is the precursor to resilience and can be developed by participating in regular, intentional activities that create positive, healthy habits of mind.

★ Just like keeping physically fit and healthy takes work, becoming mentally fit takes commitment and practise too.

★ When we embed these building blocks of mental fitness into our daily lives, we are laying a strong, solid foundation for our children's future upon which they can build the life of their dreams.

THE TEN
COMPONENTS

Young people with higher levels of wellbeing and resilience tend to be healthier, do better in school and at work, and have better relationships throughout their lives. Over the past decade, parents, carers and educators have become increasingly interested in how we can promote psychological wellbeing in our children and young people after watching them struggle to develop resilience, and instead develop escalating levels of anxiety and depression.

There is an overwhelming amount of information and advice available to parents these days, much of it conflicting, about how to best raise our kids and it is often difficult to decipher exactly how we can set them up for positive mental health. A national survey, undertaken by Zero to Three in the United States, found that 83% of parents believed that good parenting could be learned and said that if they knew more positive parenting strategies, they would use them.

For the past twenty years, scientists around the world have been studying the building blocks of mental health and wellbeing. The field of positive psychology has employed empirical research to increase our understanding of the key elements that foster positive mental health and wellbeing. Scientists have identified what people with high levels of wellbeing and positive mental health are doing to ensure they thrive and what those with less than optimal mental health and wellbeing can do to move towards thriving. The good news is that we can all learn and develop these skills and mindsets throughout our lives.

Raising a Mentally Fit Generation explores how these skills and concepts can be cultivated in childhood. It has been designed to extend your understanding of the key elements science has shown that build your child's mental fitness and to offer practical actions you can implement which will have the most impact on their wellbeing.

If we can embed these mindsets, skills and practices into our children's daily lives so they become second nature, I firmly believe that we can reduce the amount of anxiety, depression, self-harm and suicide that is significantly impacting an entire generation of children and young people.

CHAPTER ONE
Teaching brain basics

Although neuroscience lessons may seem more appropriate for medical school students than pre-schoolers, even young children are capable of understanding basic concepts about their brain.

> Teaching kids about their brain provides them with a strong foundation they can use to build their mental fitness muscles, as understanding how their brain works is the cornerstone of developing emotional intelligence and resilience.

When we teach our kids about their brain, we need to make sure it's age-appropriate information, simple to understand, and most of all, fun. You can start by sharing these five big ideas.

Number one: Our brain is the boss

Most children have an image of their brain as a squishy thing that's inside their head and is used for thinking stuff, but that's only a small part of what our brain does. Explain to your child that our brains are the boss of our entire body and control everything we do – breathing, digesting food, making faces, feeling different emotions like being happy, sad or grumpy and lots of other important things that keep us alive. Then explain how the brain is attached to the spinal cord, which is connected to all the nerves in our body and that our body is sending our brain messages all the time. When we touch something hot, the nerves in our fingers send messages up our spinal cord to our brain. Our brain gets the message it's hot and keeps us safe by sending a message back down telling us to move our hand away from the object.

I often use the hand model of the brain described by Dan Siegel and Tina Bryson, in their book *The Whole-Brain Child* to illustrate how our brain works for kids. I hold my arm up with my thumb tucked into my palm, and the other four fingers curled over the thumb. I explain that my arm is the spinal cord, that the base of my palm is the lower part of our brain where we carry and keep our feelings and that the four curled-over fingers are the higher part of our brain, the thinking part (I call it our wise leader). Then I uncurl my fingers so they can see my thumb and explain that this part of our brains is like a security guard that keeps us safe. That when it gets scared, anxious or frightened and thinks we are not safe, it will take over and tell our wise leader to take a break, and so we flip our lids (fingers flip upwards). I explain what it feels like when the wise leader is in control and what it might feel like when the security guard is in control, and then ask the kids to tell me where they think their brain is right now. I can then scaffold how they can switch their brains back to having the wise leader in control and not having a flipped lid, because we can be the boss of our brains by knowing how they work.

Number two: We need to keep our brains healthy

When we take good care of our bodies, we are taking care of our brains at the same time.

A leading Australian researcher, Dr Felice Jacka from Deakin University, and her team have revealed that eating junk food can impact the areas of the brain linked with both learning and memory as well as compounding the possibility of psychological problems developing. Dr Jacka and her team have been collecting a significant amount of evidence that indicates our diet is as important to our brain and mental health as it is to our physical health. Therefore, one of the best ways to help your kids develop mental fitness and take care of both their body and brain is with good food.

The benefits for the body of eating fresh, healthy food have long been recognised, but researchers are now also identifying foods that keep the brain healthy and improve our mental health and wellbeing. Both our bodies and brains require water to survive – our body is 60 per cent water, and our brain tissue is 80 per cent water. We need to help our kids develop the habit of regularly drinking water. I often found their drink bottles were lost or forgotten, so I used to remind the kids to have at least eight drinks from the drinking fountains each day – even if it was only a mouthful or two, for at least they were keeping hydrated.

> Sleep is as essential to both our physical and mental health and wellbeing as food and water.

It helps foster resilience and keeps our bodies and minds performing optimally. Consistent sleep deprivation can lead to obesity, poor immune function, diabetes, anxiety and depression. As one of the leading sleep researchers, Dr Robert Stickgold, a professor of psychiatry at Harvard, has said – if you don't get enough sleep you end up fat, sick and stupid.

> Regular exercise and physical activity help reduce, manage or even prevent stress, anxiety and depression. They also help our brains function better and are a crucial pillar of mental fitness for both adults and children.

Number three: Our brain is like a house

Another idea I gleaned from *The Whole-Brain Child* for explaining our brains to children was the idea that it's a house that has an upstairs part and a downstairs part. The upstairs part is where our thinking brain lives, and it helps us be creative, flexible, calm and to problem-solve. The downstairs part is where our feeling brain lives, and that is focused on keeping us safe and making sure we can run, fight or hide when there is danger. The upstairs part is similar to the wise leader, the downstairs part is like the security guard as mentioned earlier.

The upstairs and downstairs are connected by a set of stairs where lots of messages go up and down and that helps our brains to work well and calm themselves down, get along with people or think of new ideas for stories to tell. Sometimes the downstairs brain takes over when it thinks there's danger and it takes charge – telling the upstairs brain they can take a rest till the danger is gone. When the stairs connecting the two no longer work, the brain flips its lid.

I explain that this can happen to everyone – mums, dads, teachers and kids, and provide age-appropriate examples of when it's happened to me. For example, "Remember when I was running late, and I couldn't find my handbag? I kept looking in all the same places because my downstairs brain had taken over and my upstairs brain wasn't working properly." This concept of a house gives us a common language to use with our kids and helps them learn how to manage their emotions and keep their brains working well. Children need to understand how their brain is driving their emotions so they can manage what the downstairs emotional part of their brain is telling them.

Number four: Our brain can change

It is easy for kids to see that they are growing taller and that their hair is getting longer, but it's harder for them to understand that their brains change too. We need to teach our children that their brains are growing and changing every day. We can explain that people aren't born with a set amount of intelligence or skills that stay the same throughout their lives. They can learn that even though the brain is not a muscle we can help it become stronger, like we can work at making our muscles stronger, by trying new things, learning to play an instrument or sport, learning a different language or a new skill. I have found that this information about making their brains stronger can help kids as young as four and five stay motivated and keep trying when things are challenging.

Number five: We all have different brains

One of the most important things to teach children is that different people have different brains. It's important to understand that although brains work in similar ways, each person has a brain that's unique to them, and they have their own thoughts and feelings that might be different to ours. This discussion also provides the opportunity to develop their understanding that each person has their own special talents and skills and that no one is better or worse, just different, and that's okay.

Teaching our children about how their brain works empowers them to learn how to control their brain, manage their feelings and control their actions rather than feeling overwhelmed.

They can identify which part of their brain is reacting and use strategies to handle the big emotions they are feeling.

1. EXPLORE THE NERVOUS SYSTEM

Trace around your child on some butcher's paper and then help them fill in the nervous system of their body – their nerves, spinal cord and brain. Ask them to pretend that they touched something sharp with their hand and trace the path of where the message would travel from the brain and back again to the hand.

2. FUN BRAIN QUIZ

Draw up four columns on a piece of paper with the heading **My Brain** at the top. In the first column write **Has**, in the second column write **Is**, in the third column write **Can** and in the fourth column write **Needs**. Write – **these things to stay healthy** – underneath. Then ask your kids to fill out each column or tell you things that fit in each column. For example, my brain *has* lots of parts that work together to keep me safe, my brain *needs* at least eight hours' sleep, my brain *is* learning new things all the time or my brain *can* tell when I touch something hot.

3. MEMORY GAMES

Show your children a number of different objects and ask them to remember as many as possible. They have only one minute to look at them. Hide the objects after one minute has passed. Then ask them to write down on a sheet of paper, or tell you (depending on their age), as many things as they can remember. Explain that playing these types of games is like exercise for their brains.

4. BRAIN SAFETY EXPERIMENT

For this experiment you'll need two raw eggs, two tissues, two rubber bands, two sealable plastic sandwich bags, a brick, paper towels, and a box or container that is filled with bubble wrap, tissue paper or other soft material (a minimum of 20cm padding).

Place the brick and the container side by side in the middle of the room, with the paper towel underneath the brick. Ask your child to carefully draw a face on both eggs. Explain that the egg represents our head and that the shell is fragile like our skull. Discuss the importance of wearing a helmet when they ride their bikes so they can protect their brains. Gently wrap one of the eggs in two tissues and then secure the tissues with the two rubber bands. Then place that egg into one of the sandwich bags, place the other egg into the other sandwich bag and seal them.

Ask your child to drop the bag with the wrapped egg into the container with the soft material in it, and then drop the other bag onto the brick. Discuss the outcomes and how it shows us how delicate our skulls and brains are and how important it is to wear bike helmets that protect and cushion our heads in case we were in an accident.

5. CELEBRATE DIFFERENT BRAINS

Together with your child think of family members or friends you know and all of the things they are good at – and there could also be things they are not so good at. Draw an outline of a brain and then write these skills and talents on the outline. Celebrate how wonderful it is that we all have different brains that contribute to making the world the special place it is. Ensure you reinforce that no one brain is better than any other – they are simply different, learn differently and sometimes think differently to us, and that is okay.

Areas for reflection

1. Think back to the last time you didn't get enough sleep – how did that make you feel? What impact did it have on your interactions with other people? Take time to imagine how not getting enough sleep feels like for your kids.

2. What we eat affects how our brains function and how we feel. Are you and your children receiving the right nutrition and enough water to keep your brains in tip-top shape?

3. Do you have an understanding of how the brain works? Review the concept of the brain as a house with upstairs and downstairs parts and ask yourself – can I do this with my kids? Would this be useful for us as a family?

IN A NUTSHELL

★ Teaching our children about how their brain works gives them the opportunity to understand what is going on in their brains, especially when they are feeling big emotions, and to recognise what they can do when they feel like they might be flipping their lids.

★ There are fundamental things that we all need to keep our brains healthy – good quality food, enough water to drink, enough sleep, and regular physical activity and exercise. As parents, it's our job to ensure our children are provided with these basic building blocks of brain health.

★ Research in the field of neuroscience has shown that we can strengthen our brains and they can grow just like a muscle by trying new things. When things feel hard, that is a signal our brain is growing, making new connections and creating new pathways.

CHAPTER TWO
Cultivating optimism

Every day I send my kids out the door to school with this admonition 'you can choose to be happy'.

Michael J Fox

During my teaching career, I often had to coach the softball team and hold tryouts to select who would make it on to the team that year. These tryouts provided me with many opportunities to observe how my students viewed themselves, the world, and how they responded when things didn't work out as they expected. Two of my students, Jenny and Rachel, tried out and didn't make it on to the team. Both felt disappointed, but each handled it quite differently.

Jenny, who had a more optimistic way of thinking, acknowledged that there were a lot of really good players that tried out for the team and there were only 10 spaces. She thanked me for the opportunity to try out and explained that she was going to work on the things I'd suggested so that she would have a better chance of making it on to the team next year. Whereas Rachel, who had a more pessimistic way of thinking, was dejected. She commented, "No wonder I didn't get on the team, I was the worst girl at tryouts today and don't know why I bothered. I'm not that sporty anyway – I'll never make it on to the team."

Scientists have spent the past four decades studying people who think positively.

> This research has shown that optimism is a valuable psychological resource that both adults and children can learn and develop even if their outlook and attitude are inclined to be more pessimistic.

Optimism and pessimism are different ways of thinking about the world and explaining things that happen. Each of us has habitual ways of thinking about what causes things to happen. Optimists tend to take a positive view of life, expect the best outcome, and believe that they have the ability to cause positive things to happen through their effort and skills. They view setbacks as temporary and know they can do something about changing the outcome next time, like Jenny's response to the softball tryouts. Whereas people with a more pessimistic outlook tend to focus on the negative aspect of a situation, on what might go wrong, and frequently exaggerate the negative aspects of a situation. They are more likely to consider setbacks as permanent situations that are going to negatively impact on all areas of their lives and believe that there is nothing they can do to change the outcome, illustrated by Rachel's response to the softball tryouts.

We are naturally pessimistic due to our negativity bias, the negative emotions which serve to alert us to potential threats and dangers. This negative disposition has an important evolutionary biological basis. It's our own personal safety system that alerts us to when there are threats and things that are going wrong. We can almost automatically identify what's wrong faster and more frequently than what's right and going well.

I'm not suggesting that we simply ignore our problems and stick our heads in the sand pretending that everything is picture-perfect – that's not what optimists do. They also don't try to eradicate all of their negative thoughts, as thinking about what might possibly go wrong can help them avoid risky behaviours and placing themselves in dangerous situations. When things do go wrong, or challenges arise, they acknowledge that things have gone differently to the way they wanted them to and that they are disappointed, but they don't dwell on the negative aspects of the situation and blame themselves.

> Optimists acknowledge that there are going to be problems and bumps in the road and set about identifying what actions they can take to navigate these challenges.

They also recognise and accept that some things cannot be changed, are realistic in their outlook, and focus on doing what they can to achieve their goals.

Researchers have found that optimistic people have a distinct advantage when it comes to their levels of happiness and wellbeing. Compared to people who are more pessimistic, optimists are:

* more successful at school and work

* less anxious

* more resilient and better able to cope with negative events

* less likely to suffer depression

* physically and mentally healthier

* living longer.

As Dr Martin Seligman points out in his books *Learned Optimism* and *The Optimistic Child*, one of the best things parents and teachers can do for kids is to help them develop an optimistic mindset.

In 2003 I was fortunate enough to study with Dr Martin Seligman, commonly considered to be the father of positive psychology. Dr Seligman had spent the past three decades investigating optimism and happiness. I asked him about possible ways we could stem the rising tide of depression and anxiety we were seeing in schools. He explained that as adults we could help children challenge negative self-talk, which would go a long way in addressing these problems.

When children feel that they have a secure base in their parents, they develop trust in the world and tend to believe that the world is a good place. This fosters an optimistic mindset that allows them to explore, take risks, develop confidence in their own abilities, and feel hopeful about the future.

It's also important to be very careful with how you provide criticism to young children. When they are little, children take criticism to heart completely, and this can shape both their beliefs about themselves and their explanatory style. If children receive frequent and wide-ranging criticism, they are more likely to form a pessimistic self-image.

Parents are vital to their child developing an optimistic personal explanatory style in their early years. Children are very attuned to their parent's explanatory styles (optimistic or pessimistic) as well as those of their teachers, extended family members, and their favourite characters in cartoons, movies, or books. Whether it's Dory from *Finding Nemo*, Olaf from *Frozen*, Sponge Bob Squarepants, Winnie the Pooh, Happy the Dwarf, Goofy, The Roadrunner or Joy from *Inside Out* there are plenty of optimistic characters they can emulate.

Children watch everything we do, keenly observing how we think about and respond to different situations. Modelling optimistic behaviours is a crucial way you can help them develop an optimistic mindset.

Sometimes things don't turn out so well, and in these situations what matters is how kids make sense of the situation or the unwanted outcome. As parents, we need to help guide them from global, personal assessments to more specific, situational ones. For example, "I failed the test because I'm stupid and I'll never be good at science" is a pessimistic response. Whereas "I failed because I didn't understand the problems and need more practice" demonstrates an optimistic mindset that shows they have a plan of action to make the outcome different next time.

When you hear your child say pessimistic things, even in an offhand way, gently confront them about it. When they think pessimistic thoughts, when they expect bad things to happen; they are priming their brains for these things to occur. A pessimist thinks in catastrophic ways like, "I'm never going to make friends at this new school. No one talks to me, and no one is ever going to like me."

To challenge your child's pessimism, you need to recognise the following three negative thought patterns that lead to pessimistic thinking:

* **Permanence:** This always happens and always will
* **Pervasive:** Nothing ever goes right
* **Personal:** This always happens to me.

If you hear them using phrases like these, call them out, challenge their thinking and help them dispute their catastrophic thinking.

Observe how you speak about your life and the discussions and comments your children hear. Highlight the good aspects of experiences and situations and if something doesn't work out, explain it in ways that are specific and allow for a different outcome next time.

The way we foster optimism in infants and toddlers is significantly different from what we do with older children because young children don't have the intellectual skills to recognise, monitor and dispute their thoughts or self-talk.

> We need to surround them with love and positivity as well as provide them with developmentally appropriate challenges so they can experience mastery.

This gaining of mastery is foundational to developing an optimistic outlook on the world. Children gain mastery when they feel that they can control situations because their behaviour causes certain outcomes. I observed a young mother doing this with her toddler in a restaurant. The toddler banged her hands on her highchair tray and then looked at her mother. The mum then clapped her hands together, and the toddler giggled and banged her hands on the tray again. Her mother responded in the same way – then the toddler banged three times, with the mother responding the same way. This allowed the child to understand that she was able to control the actions of her mother and gave her a sense of mastery. Another way this occurs is when parents or early childhood educators' scaffold more difficult tasks by breaking them down into steps they know the young children will be able to master. There can also be opportunities for mastery in the kitchen – little ones could help mix a cake, unpack groceries, place ingredients in the blender for smoothies. When you're reading together, encourage them to point at pictures they are interested in and then talk with them about that picture. There are a wide variety of experiences that provide opportunities for our children to experience mastery and develop the foundations of optimism.

1. MONITOR KIDS' SELF-TALK

Start helping your child understand the concept of self-talk, by explaining that we all have a little voice that chatters away constantly to us in our heads. This begins in the second or third year of life, around the same time children begin talking in sentences. Listen for what they are saying to themselves as the majority of their words are said aloud at this age – until age five when they start to internalise it and keep it to themselves. Explain to your child that this internal dialogue can be our best supporter or worst enemy and ask them whether they want a supporter or enemy. Kids frequently communicate their negative thoughts out loud – "I'm useless at sports, and no one is going to choose me to be on the team" or "my hair is so ugly". Support your child in recognising their harsh negative thoughts and internal dialogue. Help them to stop these by discussing the thoughts with them. Suggest that they can become a detective who recognises their negative beliefs which set them up to feel bad, and then scaffold how they can change these thoughts to something more helpful.

They could do this by labelling those negative thoughts as coming from their mean, unkind negative brain. Let them know that they are the boss of their brain and thoughts, and they can change them by asking themselves questions like:

★ How true is this thought?

★   Am I being mean to myself?

★   Is it helpful to think this way? And what can I think instead?

You could even have them write their mean negative thoughts down onto a piece of paper, then scrunch it up and throw it away. Then replace it with a more kind and helpful thought.

2. CHANGING EXPLANATIONS FOR ADVERSITY

The next time your child fails a test, doesn't score during a sporting game or isn't invited to a friend's house, support them by changing their explanation for the event. Gently ask questions such as:

★   What other explanations can you think of?

★   How much did the behaviour of other people contribute to the situation?

★   What can you do differently next time?

3. PROBLEM METER

You can help your child gain perspective by giving their worries a score out of ten, on how important the problem really is. Draw a semi-circle on a piece of paper then divide this into thirds with one coloured in green, one yellow and one red. Mark the green section with the numbers 1–4 (with 4 is on the line between green and yellow) then mark the yellow section with the numbers 5–7 (with 7 on the line between yellow and red) and the red section is marked with 8–10. This is similar to a fire safety warning system. Ranking their problems helps children gauge their reactions.

You need to establish points of reference for each number from 1 to 10 on this problem/disaster meter. Draw from children's past experiences, for example, a score of 1 out of 10 may be losing your sock. A score of 10 out of 10 may be linked to when a pet or grandparent died. The colours can help children realise the seriousness of the problem and the tool can be used as a reality check when they overreact to negative or bad events.

4. UNFORTUNATELY/FORTUNATELY GAME

To help switch a child's lens from pessimistic/negative thinking to a more optimistic style you can play the game Unfortunately/ Fortunately. You think of a tricky situation – so you say, "Unfortunately, the shop ran out of popcorn." Then your child says, "Fortunately, they sold ice cream." Then you say, "Unfortunately they didn't have any chocolate ice cream," and you continue for as long as you can. The best way to do this is for you to start the game with Unfortunately- so your child has to think of the positives.

5. ACKNOWLEDGING THE POSITIVES IN LIFE

Encourage your children to notice and acknowledge the good things that happen to them, things that have gone well for them, others who are kind and friendly, both their own and other people's strengths and things they are good at. Talk with your kids about good things that have happened that day at dinner-time and ask them to describe how they felt – you can join in with this, too. You could ask younger children what made them smile today.

Areas for reflection

1. What are your beliefs about optimism and pessimism? Have you ever been labelled as an optimist or pessimist?

2. Are you aware of your own explanatory style? Does it lead to a more optimistic or pessimistic outlook? What is this modelling for your children?

3. Stop and think of the last time your child experienced an unwanted outcome. How did they make sense of the unwanted outcome? Can you see ways in which you could help them change their explanation for the event to a more optimistic response?

IN A NUTSHELL

★   Optimism and pessimism are explanatory styles we use to explain negative events that occur in our lives.

★   Optimists see problems as temporary, specific to a situation and caused by external circumstances. Pessimists see problems as permanent, universal (going across many areas of their lives) and blame themselves. We are naturally pessimistic due to our negativity bias but can overcome this by paying deliberate attention to positive things in our lives.

★   Your explanatory style is learned, both pessimism and optimism are habits of thinking, and it is possible to change your outlook and explanatory style.

CHAPTER THREE
Managing emotions

Children with higher levels of emotional intelligence enjoy increased self-confidence, better performance in school, better physical health and healthier social relationships.

John Gottman

It was 4:30 in the afternoon, and I'd taken Mitchell, who was eight at the time, shopping after school. Both he and I were tired, but I needed to pick something up from the store before they closed at 5. I was in a rush, and he'd stopped to look at a toy he wanted me to buy. I explained that we weren't toy shopping today and that he needed to hurry up as the store was closing soon. This started a tantrum that lasted for a good 10 minutes. There were tears and snot all over his face as well as angry words from him – I just didn't care about him and I was the worst person in the world. He completely lost it in a meltdown of epic proportions.

I was embarrassed by the scene he was making and struggled to calm him down. Everything I said seemed to make matters worse, and our exhaustion only added fuel to an already raging fire. I admit that I wasn't using the best strategies to deal with the situation at the time, which eventually led to both of us losing our tempers. It was far from my finest moment, and as I was driving home, I knew I hadn't been a good role model of self-regulation at all. I apologised to Mitchell for getting angry and using an unkind voice. I wanted to make sure our shopping trips never resembled a scene from a *Mad Max* movie again and recognised that I needed to model healthy ways of handling my negative emotions even when I was tired.

We all experience anger, fear, frustration, sadness, rejection, disappointment, jealousy and guilt at different times; they are simply part of being human.

> **Mentally fit people can label their emotions and manage their emotional reactions to external events and strong feelings without yelling, throwing things or damaging property.**

They can express a broad range of emotions and don't get stuck in any one particular emotion for great lengths of time. While they might feel angry, frustrated, sad, anxious or scared, these feelings don't prevent them from managing the situation well as they have developed emotional agility.

As a guidance officer, I encouraged the students I was working with to identify and express what they were thinking and feeling, and to consider the thoughts and feelings of other students in their class. The results were often extraordinary. Kids as young as seven were very self-aware, making statements such as:

* "I don't like it and get angry when my friends don't want to play with me – I yell at them to try and get them to understand, but it only makes things worse."

* "I feel incredibly anxious in class because I'm worried that I am going to be slower than my friends at the work, and they might make fun of me."

* "I get angry when Mum and Dad work all the time and can't help me with my school stuff or take me to soccer. It makes me want to throw things, but I don't 'cos then they'd get mad."

After working with thousands of families, I came to realise that as adults, we frequently underestimate our kid's ability to process and understand complex emotions. We think they're less capable and try to protect them from the unpleasant, thornier subjects and don't bring these up or discuss them.

As soon as they begin talking, we can teach our kids how to identify and talk about their feelings.

If we create safe environments where children can openly talk about their feelings and trust that they will be listened to and not judged, most kids will talk freely about their feelings. Children can hold mature conversations about their emotions if we explicitly teach them the skills and language they need.

Research from the Yale Centre for Emotional Intelligence has shown that emotional intelligence, sometimes shortened to EQ, 'predicts over 54 per cent of the variation in success in people's relationships, quality of life, long-term health and effectiveness at work and school.' This is reflected in the fact that children and young people with high EQ stay in school longer, receive better grades, make healthier choices than their peers who have lower levels of EQ, and are less likely to end up in jail. By teaching our kids how to recognise their feelings, understand where they come from and how to deal with them, we are providing them with some of the most crucial skills for happiness and success throughout their lives.

In another study, researchers from Penn State and Duke University interviewed kindergarten teachers about children's social and emotional skills – how well they shared, listened to others, resolved problems with their friends and were helpful.

The researchers followed these children until they were young adults to investigate what happened to them. They discovered that the children with the highest social and emotional competency scores in kindergarten functioned better overall. They were twice as likely to obtain a university degree and more likely to have full-time jobs by age 25. The children who had trouble cooperating, listening and resolving conflict were more likely to drop out of high school, have legal problems and substance abuse issues. For every one-point decline in social competencies at age five, a child had a 67 per cent higher possibility of being arrested in early adulthood, a 52 per cent higher possibility of binge drinking, and an 82 per cent higher probability of living in public housing (or at least being on the waitlist). These results were independent of the effects of ethnicity, being born to teenage parents, poverty or family stressors.

> As children grow, they learn different social and emotional skills at different rates – there is no one linear model to summarize how emotional intelligence should look in children of different ages.

Please don't panic if your child is already older than five – the good news is the skills of emotional intelligence can be taught, and children can learn them at any age. Daniel Goleman has identified four components of emotional intelligence: self-awareness, self-management, social awareness and relationship management.

Self-awareness is the ability to identify and understand your own emotions. To become self-aware, it's essential that children can observe, recognise and name their emotions, notice different emotional reactions they have, and then understand the relationship between the emotions they are feeling and the ways they behave. They also need to develop an understanding of how their own actions, moods and emotions impact other people.

Self-management enables us to regulate and manage how we react to our emotions. This does not mean that we expect children to hide their true feelings or not express their emotions. We need to help them understand that there is a right time, place and appropriate way to express their emotions and impulses so they can stay in control and not physically or verbally lash out at others.

Social awareness is our ability to understand how other people are feeling. It requires us to recognise other people's emotions and then respond to them in appropriate ways based on this information. For example, when your child recognises that their friend is feeling sad, this influences how they respond to that person, and they may choose to do something that cheers them up or helps them feel better.

Relationship management is our children's ability to interact well with others and manage their social relationships.

> When children understand their own emotions, as well as the feelings of others, they can then apply this information when they are communicating and interacting with other people.

This helps them build and manage relationships and connections with people they encounter every day.

One of the ways parents can help kids develop self-awareness, self-management, social awareness and relationship management is through Professor John Gottman's Emotion Coaching approach. Professor Gottman developed this approach after analysing the parenting of hundreds of couples with children aged four or five. He gave them questionnaires, conducted thousands of hours of interviews, observed their behaviour in his lab, videotaped sessions of the children playing with their best friends, monitored their heart rates, respiration, blood flow and sweating as well as taking urine samples from the children to measure stress-related hormones. He continued to follow the development and progress of these children through adolescence, conducting more interviews and observations. The children with parents who used emotion coaching techniques were able to calm themselves faster (their heart rates slowed much more quickly than their peers), they related to their friends better, had more focused attention, and could manage tough social situations in later childhood like getting bullied and teased.

There are five crucial steps to emotion coaching.

1. Being aware of children's emotions

As parents, we need to be aware of both our own and our children's emotions. We need to be able to recognise what we are feeling and be sensitive to what others, especially our children, are feeling. Feelings frequently precede outbursts of behaviour, so it is better if we can detect when our children are struggling and help them manage their feelings before they lose control.

> Our kids may not even be aware of how they're feeling when they are really little, so noticing what's going on for them and being aware of how they're feeling can prevent World War Three from breaking out.

This step is very similar to Goleman's first component of EQ where we are helping our children understand that emotions are a natural and valuable part of life that provides them with information they can use to make decisions. Watch your children, listen to their language, note changes in facial expressions, body language or tone of voice so you can learn how they express different emotions both physically and verbally. This way, you can help your child respond to their big feelings in healthy ways and provide guidance before their emotions escalate into challenging behaviours.

Parents don't need to be afraid of showing emotions in front of their kids as long as it's done in a respectful and constructive way. When we model how to handle difficult and uncomfortable feelings effectively, our children will be better prepared for life. If we hide our emotions, our kids are less capable of handling negative, unpleasant emotions in healthy ways.

2. Viewing emotions as an opportunity for connection and teaching

Even though it seems counterintuitive, a tantrum is the best time to connect with your child and use it as a teachable moment. I admit this doesn't feel like the most rational thing to do when your child is hurling objects or verbal abuse at you, and stopping misbehaviour is the priority. However, we need to do this in a specific way, so the child knows it's about their behaviour and not them personally. For example, "We don't draw on the walls at Grandma's house", instead of "Stop being so horrendous". The children who heard phrases similar to the last one had higher levels of stress-related hormones in their bodies and had more difficulties getting along with friends.

> When our children encounter challenging situations like not wanting to share a toy, falling out with a friend, a bad grade on a test, being teased or not being selected for a sporting team, it is a wonderful opportunity to connect with them, demonstrate empathy for how they are feeling and teach them ways to handle those difficult feelings.

This way, we can demonstrate to our children that we care and that we are on their side, an ally that will help them figure out how to solve their problem.

When we're feeling upset about something, we don't like it if people tell us to get over it or that we shouldn't be feeling that way. Children don't like it either. All our emotions have a reason for being there, and we need to give our kids the time and space to feel their feelings without trying to change them. Experiencing feelings and moving through them is crucial to letting them go. The next time your child feels upset because something has gone wrong in a game or on the playground, tell them, "It's okay to feel disappointed. I'll sit here with you so you can feel it until it passes."

3. Listening empathetically and validating feelings

When we listen empathetically to our children's concerns, we are showing them that we respect them, take their emotions seriously, and understand how they are feeling. We need to avoid judging or criticising our children's emotions or saying things like, "You shouldn't feel that way" or "Everything is going to be fine" as these are dismissive statements. They don't work with adults when we are highly emotional, and they certainly won't work with our kids. Instead, we need to validate their feelings and show them we understand and are on their side. We don't have to accept or validate their behaviour if it's inappropriate, but we do need to demonstrate our care and empathy for them. You can do this by saying something simple like, "I noticed you were frowning when I mentioned going swimming at school today" and then wait for their response. Once they start opening up, we can help them find ways to understand, label and cope with their uncomfortable feelings.

4. Helping the child verbally label emotions

When children can label their emotions and talk about the big scary feelings they're having, these will dissipate more quickly. As adults, we have the words to describe our feelings; our children don't. We need to help them develop a broad emotional vocabulary so they can label the feelings they're experiencing. Dan Siegel in his book *The Whole-Brain Child* has shown that when people can describe and label their intense feelings, this calms their nervous system and helps them recover from upsetting situations or incidents more quickly. Putting their feelings into words helps children define what's happening for them and helps transform big, scary, overwhelming feelings into something that other people feel too and that can be managed (with some guidance and help at first).

5. Setting limits while helping the child problem-solve

Once we have acknowledged the emotion that sits behind the tantrum or other challenging inappropriate behaviour and have helped our children label it, we then need to ensure our children understand that some behaviours are inappropriate and will not be tolerated.

All feelings are acceptable — but all behaviour is not.

Every emotion is valid, though we need to make it very clear that angry feelings are okay but violent, destructive and aggressive behaviour is not. We have every right to set limits, and we need to set limits to ensure our children know what is socially acceptable. You need to be firm and guide your child into considering more appropriate ways to manage their negative feelings. For example, you might say something like, "You're mad at Jenny because she took that doll from you. I would be upset and angry too. But it's not okay for you to pull her hair. What could you do instead?" We need to model appropriate ways to deal with big emotions and teach them specific strategies and tools they can use. You have listened empathetically, helped her label her feelings, and set limits on her misbehaviour – now it's time to help her develop problem-solving skills, as you won't always be there to solve the problem. We need to provide scaffolding and guidance for our kids to come up with ideas about possible solutions that are effective and consider other people's feelings.

When you observe your child processing something emotional, which is frequently a slower process for kids, acknowledge what you're observing and praise their efforts. If you notice them taking some deep breaths and doing the activity that scares them, where they might once have avoided it or run away, or if they went outside and had a jump on the trampoline instead of hitting their sibling who'd wrecked their Lego creation, acknowledge their behaviour accordingly and praise their efforts. This provides them with positive feedback, and a dopamine hit that lights up the brain, for making a healthy choice.

Please don't put unrealistic expectations on yourself about following these five steps all the time; it's not always an option or practical to do this in the heat of the moment. Dr Gottman discovered that even if parents only do all five steps 20–25 per cent of the time, this still provides children with a strong foundation of EQ skills that will benefit them for the rest of their life.

> **Children need to experience the kaleidoscope of human emotions in order to develop emotional wellbeing and resilience.**

If they don't experience what it's like to be disappointed or sad, they are unlikely to develop the skills to manage those feelings or the ability to empathise with others. However, due to our innate negativity bias, the negative emotions which serve to alert us to potential threats and dangers far outnumber the positive emotions we experience. This is especially true in childhood, when our emotional awareness is amplified for possible threats. This can trigger children's protective emotions to become overactive, which flood their bodies with the stress hormones adrenaline and cortisol and can leave their stress response permanently switched on. When this happens, there is a greater chance of them developing anxiety disorders and other emotional problems.

Professor Barbara Fredrickson and her colleagues at the University of North Carolina found that positive emotions undo the effects of stress and turn off the stress response by replacing the stress hormones with serotonin and dopamine. This calms us physically and fuels our prefrontal cortex (the thinking part of our brain), enabling us to think more clearly and make effective, rational decisions. Fredrickson asserts that positive emotions are vital to our emotional wellbeing and mental health.

When children experience positive emotions such as love, gratitude, optimism, hope, contentment, kindness, enthusiasm and confidence, it has a powerful impact on their wellbeing and fosters an inner calm and positivity. It's therefore critically important that we help children experience and build positive emotions on a daily basis so that they learn how to generate their own positivity and create a positive balance of emotions that builds lasting resilience and wellbeing.

1. SHARE YOUR FEELINGS

All of us experience a wide variety of emotions – frustration, disappointment, anger, fear, sadness, jealousy, happiness and it's a good idea to share these with your children whenever it's appropriate to do so. We don't want to burden our kids with our grown-up emotions and experiences, but we do want them to understand that even we feel those things at different times and have had to learn how to manage them.

2. FEELINGS BINOCULARS

This activity develops children's awareness about emotions, what they feel like in their bodies and can help them identify emotions they are feeling. You will need two cardboard rolls, some glue to stick them together, some pens to decorate them with and possibly some string if you'd like your children to hang them around their neck. Talk to your child about how binoculars work and describe how they can allow things to be seen up close. Then explain that you are going to make a pair of binoculars that allows them to look inside their bodies and see how they are feeling. Once the binoculars are finished, model how to use them by using them on yourself – looking at your feet first and then moving up your body to explain what you notice in your body and naming how you feel. Then your child can have a go and see what they find with the binoculars. If they are having trouble identifying what is happening in their bodies, talk about other examples when you have used your binoculars to notice when your tummy was feeling upset and your heart was pounding because you were nervous about an important meeting.

3. EMOTION SQUEEZE BALLS

These balls help children identify the facial expressions that represent different feelings. You'll need yellow balloons, permanent markers, rice and a funnel.

To draw the facial expressions of different emotions on the balloons, you'll need to blow them up a little bit and hold the end so the air doesn't come out. Then talk with your child about what facial expressions match different emotions and see if they can guess which one you're drawing on the balloon. Once you've drawn the face let it dry for several minutes and then put the funnel in the open neck of the balloon. Pour the rice into the balloon to fill it, leaving the neck section free so you can tie a knot.

Keep them in a container your child can access and they can select which emotion they are feeling at the time based on the facial expression – they can also be used as stress balls and fidget toys.

4. ENERGY THERMOMETER

This activity will help your child notice how much energy they have inside, what they are feeling and how they can manage their energy. Draw a picture of a temperature gauge or thermometer, with a picture of a fish at the bottom and a volcano at the top. Then ask your child if they feel calm like the fish swimming in the water or explosive like the volcano. Talk about how different feelings can make their body have different levels of energy, and brainstorm ways they can feel more like the calm fish. This could be doing things like going outside and running around, deep belly breathing, colouring in or listening to music.

5. IDENTIFY HEALTHY COPING STRATEGIES

Your child should know that it is possible for people to lose control; however, we need to help them identify different coping strategies they can utilise when they need to regain control. It's important to make sure that you identify appropriate coping strategies for your child as each child is different and will need different methods to help them calm down. Some coping strategies that might be useful are: listening to music, colouring-in or drawing, going to a quiet space to chill, squeezing a stress ball, jumping on a trampoline, blowing bubbles, drinking a glass of cold water, punching a pillow, kicking a ball outside, going for a run-around, scribbling on a piece of paper or ripping paper up. Once you have identified them together, you can talk about how they can use them when they need them both at home and school.

You can also make some visual reminders of the strategies and ideas by placing photos of the activities on small laminated cards and having them stuck on the fridge or threaded on to a keyring they could carry in their pocket, so they have a reminder of these healthy coping strategies when they start to feel their emotions escalate.

Children learn by watching their parents and other significant adults in their lives and are quick to pick up and mimic behaviours, either positive or negative, that they have seen exhibited. It's vital, therefore that we are good role models and practise what we preach. We are human and can become upset; when that happens, acknowledge it and then demonstrate how you use your coping strategies to regain control and work through the situation.

Areas for reflection

1. Take a moment and list all the different emotions you can think of – how many would you describe as positive, how many negative? Which do you experience most?

2. When you become frustrated, angry or disappointed with your children, what's your typical response? What is this modelling for them?

3. Review the five steps of emotion coaching above and ask yourself – can I do this with my kids? Would it work for me? How can I make it a priority?

IN A NUTSHELL

★ All emotions serve a useful purpose in our lives, both positive and negative. Our emotions are simply data telling us something about the experiences we are currently having. They are signs that something is right or wrong in our world and help us communicate that to others around us.

★ The primary pathways in the brain that enable us to recognise, understand and manage our emotions are formed in early childhood. These are substantially impacted by parent-child interactions and children's observations of the ways their parents manage their emotions and regulate their behaviour. As parents, we need to nurture our children's positive emotions on a daily basis so that we are creating a positive balance of emotions in their lives.

★ We need to explicitly teach our kids the skills of emotional intelligence – how to recognise their feelings, understand where they come from, and how to deal with them. This will help them regulate their behaviour, develop emotional agility and navigate social complexities.

CHAPTER FOUR
Recognising their strengths

Success is achieved by developing our strengths, not by eliminating our weaknesses.

Marilyn Vos Savant

When Mitchell was 11, he saw an antibullying video and talk at school. In the video, a girl sat next to an empty chair with a sign on it that said, 'sit with me'. When he arrived home, we talked about how this was an opportunity to show kindness, be inclusive and let people know they are cared for. A few weeks later, Mitchell came home and told me that he'd seen a classmate sitting by themselves at lunchtime and had remembered that the child's best friend had moved away. Mitchell decided to sit with him and start a conversation at lunchtime and was planning on inviting him to play games with Mitchell's friends the following day. Mitchell explained that after seeing that video and chatting with me about what

strengths he could use in these situations, he was now noticing when other kids were possibly feeling left out. He liked to
help them feel accepted and included. Some of Mitchell's top
strengths are empathy, kindness and social intelligence.

> As humans, we are very good at focusing on weaknesses and the
> negative aspects of both people and situations.

We can almost automatically identify what's wrong faster and
more frequently than what's right and going well. This negative disposition (our negativity bias) involves everyone, even
those with the sunniest of personalities, as it has an important
evolutionary biological basis. If our ancestors weren't always
on the lookout for things that could do them harm, they
wouldn't have survived. It's our own personal safety system
that alerts us to when there are threats and things that are
going wrong.

What this can lead us to as parents is focusing on our children's negative behaviours and seeing all the things they're
doing wrong. I recognised myself doing this when Mitchell
came home with his report card in high school. He had
received outstanding marks in the majority of his subjects,
but there were two Ds included in his grades. I was tired and
stressed that afternoon, and when he showed me his report
card, I placed a significant amount of focus on those two
Ds. His face fell, and I had one of those horrible moments of
parental guilt. What should have been a happy reconnection

and celebration of his achievements in six of his eight sub-jects, instead ended up being a painful experience for both of us. My focus could have been better spent sitting down with Mitch at a later time and talking about what went well in his other subjects so that we could tap into the strengths he was using there and possibly employ those patterns of behaviour in the subjects where he received Ds.

A significant amount of research has been undertaken in char-acter, or personality strengths, and the impact these have on our wellbeing and success. For the past two decades, research-ers around the globe have investigated whether there are a set of strengths that are universal. A team of scientists undertook a large-scale study using a variety of methods including:

* analysing the world's major religions for common characteristics

* identifying the strengths displayed by the heroes or positive role models in classic children's stories from different cultures

* analysing works by Socrates and Aristotle as well as other philosophers throughout history

* researching biographies of famous people and institutions.

This research was drawn together and formed the basis for the Values in Action (VIA) model which has been validated in over 50 countries around the world and is being used in organisations, schools and even professional sports teams.

> There is a general agreement that helping children and young people develop their strengths is valuable.

Professor Lea Waters has identified that developing and working with children and young people's strengths has a positive impact on their thinking processes, self-esteem, behaviour and wellbeing. Using their strengths increases their likelihood of being healthy, happy and highly engaged in learning. In adulthood, the benefits of developing and using our strengths include being healthier, having a lower risk of depression, better performance at work and even being happily married.

What are strengths?

All of us have strengths and other things we find challenging. Recognising, tapping into and building on children's strengths is one of the fundamental ways to help your children develop their mental fitness muscles. When children use their strengths on a regular basis, they have higher levels of optimism, confidence, cognitive flexibility and resilience.

Character strengths have been studied throughout history, and this has increased considerably over the past two decades.

In their book *Character strengths and virtues*, Martin Seligman and Christopher Peterson classified 24 character strengths into the following six overarching virtues:

1. **Wisdom** – creativity, curiosity, judgment, love of learning, perspective

2. **Courage** – bravery, honesty, perseverance, zest
3. **Humanity** – love, kindness, social intelligence
4. **Justice** – fairness, leadership, teamwork
5. **Temperance** – forgiveness, humility, prudence, self-regulation
6. **Transcendence** – appreciation of beauty and excellence, humour, gratitude, spirituality, hope.

Other strengths researchers such as Alex Linley, Susan Harper, Donald Clifton and James Harter explain that strengths can also be considered in these six categories:

1. **Personal strengths** – empathy, kindness, compassion, curiosity, thoughtfulness
2. **Social strengths** – being a good listener, a good friend, being truthful, following rules, resisting peer pressure, respecting personal space, comforting others
3. **Language strengths** – great communicators, both talking and listening, often captivating speakers, attentive listeners, humorous and expressive, large vocabulary, and can convey their thoughts with clarity and structure
4. **Literacy strengths** – very good reading and writing skills, vivid imaginations, strong memories, advanced vocabularies and love to read and/or write
5. **Maths and logic strengths** – strong maths and logic skills, solving puzzles and word problems, good at

sorting and organising, can do maths in their heads and enjoy taking apart and reassembling things

6. **Other strengths** – can include skills such as playing a musical instrument, playing a sport very well, from being good with younger children to shining when they volunteer their time for a good cause.

In order to be considered a strength, three significant factors need to be present. When you're looking to identify your child's strengths, remember to keep these factors in mind:

1. **Are they good at it?** – observe where your child learns things quickly, has repeated success and displays above-average aptitude and good grades

2. **Does it give them energy and help them feel good?** – observe what activities give your child energy where they seem to be full of zest for life

3. **What do they choose to do?** – observe what your child chooses to do in their free time, how they talk about that activity and how often they participate in it.

If you keep these three factors in mind, it will assist you in understanding the difference between your child's true strengths and those things that look like one of their strengths because they are good at them. Not every interest, skill or talent we have can be considered a strength. There are 'learned behaviours' that we do purely because we have to, and we can become very good at these, so they appear to be strengths.

One of the quickest ways to identify if it's a true strength is to ask yourself these questions: Is my child good at it? Do they enjoy doing it? Do they choose to do it? And does it energise them?

A true strength is something that ticks all three criteria – we're good at it, they give us energy when we do them and we are motivated to do it on our own accord.

None of us are good at everything

In society today, there's a misconception that we all need to be well-rounded, which makes many parents view their children's weaknesses as areas that require a lot of attention and improvement. This is often undertaken through constructive criticism, similar to what I heard throughout my childhood: "Too bossy, overly theatrical, always asking questions." What I came to understand was that these were strengths of leadership, organisation, curiosity, creativity and communication, all of which have stood me in very good stead throughout my adult career. We all have weaknesses, they are a normal part of life, and we need to steer clear of the trap of continually focusing on our weaknesses.

When we constantly ask our children to work on improving their weaknesses it can be incredibly tiring and disheartening, it will sap their energy, and their execution won't be nearly as proficient as when they're playing to their strengths.

After Mitchell got those two Ds on his report card we sat down several days later and examined his strengths. I helped him realise he could tap into his strengths of love of learning, perseverance and communication. Mitch loved debating and set about learning the difficult subjects in a similar way to how he developed his debating content, arguments, and analysis. It took time, but by his final year, his grades had significantly improved.

I was working within a small group with students from the third grade. One little girl started to continually ask questions, interrupting the other students learning. As a group, we tired of it very quickly. Rather than becoming upset with her, I explained that I could see persistence and curiosity were two of her highest strengths but asked her to dial them back at that time as they were interrupting other students' learning. I then asked her to use a different strength instead. After reminding her how empathetic she is, I asked her to think about how her constant questioning impacted the group and asked her to turn up the volume on consideration. This idea was drawn from Lea Water's work on Visible Wellbeing, a strengths-based approach for classrooms and schools, which I had shared with my teaching partner at the beginning of the year. Our students understood the language of strengths and how tapping into their own strengths could help them learn and be successful both in the classroom and playground. We wanted our kids to feel capable, valued and respected as this helps them develop their mental fitness muscles.

How to identify children's strengths

As a guidance counsellor, many parents asked me about the best method they could use to identify their children's strengths. There are a variety of tools to choose from for children aged 10+ that kids and parents can use together to identify what their strengths may be. For younger kids, I recommended parents undertake a process called 'strengths spotting', where parents observe their kids in a variety of different settings and interactions with different people and watch for the following clues:

* ⭐ **Favourites** – what environments or activities is your child continually drawn to?

* ⭐ **Quick learning** – what skills or activities does your child pick up easily and quickly?

* ⭐ **Gratification** – what activities is your child enthusiastic about and do these fulfil them?

* ⭐ **Loss of time** – are there any pursuits that your child becomes so engrossed in they lose track of time whenever they're participating in them?

Think back to those moments when they lit up, and you will have most probably witnessed one of their strengths in action.

Top 10 strategies for strengths

Still stuck? Here are 10 strategies, ideas and activities that can help your kids develop their strengths.

1. Choose a different character strength every week, discuss it as a family, what it looks like, how you can see it in others, and immerse your children in the language of this character strength.

2. Read books that relate to different strengths as bedtime stories (there's a list of ideas in the Resources section at the back of the book).

3. Create family traditions focused on different strengths – for example, you could practise kindness by donating time to a charity together during the holiday season or help elderly neighbours who don't have relatives close by.

4. Find movies to watch together that reinforce different strengths.

5. Strength spot together when you're out and about doing everyday activities. Ask your kids what strengths they've seen in other people – their teachers at school, their friends, other family members.

6. Play charades together – have your kids choose a strength and act it out.

7. Make something to represent a strength in a creative way – draw, paint or represent a strength in another medium.

8. Listen out for songs that help kids learn about different strengths. You can sing together and talk about the artist who sings the song and their strengths.

9. Have the strength of the week displayed on the fridge, or somewhere your kids can see it throughout the week, so they'll be reminded of what they're focusing on.

10. Catch them engaging their strengths and let them know you've noticed. For example, "I saw that you stopped and helped your sister with her chores, that was kind." This helps build their awareness of what their strengths are and what it feels like when they use them.

As parents, we can help our children learn how to identify and utilise their strengths which is one of the primary ways to build mental fitness. When both kids and adults discover their strengths, they come alive. Strengths don't make one child more special than another, as we all have different strengths that make us unique. Instead, we should help our kids celebrate our differences and develop an understanding of how other people's strengths can complement their own.

> Strengths are a positive resource a child will have for their entire lives.

When they use them, they experience higher levels of happiness, lower levels of depression, elevated levels of confidence and self-esteem and increased psychological wellbeing, which makes it well worth the effort we need to put in as parents to foster our children's strengths.

1. OBSERVE YOUR CHILDREN

Observe your children when they're playing. You'll spot how they interact with others, what activities they prefer, which ones they avoid, what new skills or activities they learn quickly, when they are most enthusiastic and excited about doing something, which activities they become so engrossed in they lose track of time, how they handle conflict or problems and the unique ways in which they perceive themselves.

2. KEEP A STRENGTHS JOURNAL

Keep a record of the things your child does and anything that indicates they may be displaying a strength. Here are some questions that can act as a guide:

★   When does your child express joy and happiness?
     What are they doing?

★   What activities keep your child's attention the longest?

★   Are they generous, kind or compassionate? How do they
     demonstrate this?

★   Are they cautious and careful, creative and curious?
     How do they demonstrate this?

3. ASK QUESTIONS

Ask your children age-appropriate questions about themselves such as:

★   What is your favourite thing to do with me?

★   When do you get most excited at school?

★   How would you describe yourself to someone?

★   What feelings made you respond like that to this situation?

★   How do you think we could solve this problem?

When they answer really listen to their language. If they use words like,"I love to…" or "It's awesome when I…" then it's likely that they are using or talking about an area of strength. Sometimes we assume we know what our kids are good at, what they're thinking and feeling because we project our own patterns of thinking, feeling and behaving on to them. We need to find out what motivates, annoys, inspires, discourages or angers them as this will provide us with clues about their strengths.

4. TRY NEW THINGS

Children need to experiment and try many things, take risks, and know that it's okay not to be good at something or to fail. This is all part of the journey to discovering their strengths and passions. The more children try new things and are free to experiment and explore different skills and activities, the easier it will be to discover their strengths and what activities energise rather than drain them. What three new experiences could you introduce to your child this week? Try a different recreational activity as a family? Draw with charcoal instead of pencils? Go to the museum instead of the playground?

5. MAKE A SHIELD OR CHAIN OF STRENGTHS

In this activity you draw the shape of a shield on cardboard and then divide it into four sections – Self, Family, Friends and School. Then encourage your child to draw or write the talents, skills and strengths they have in each of these areas. This then becomes their shield of strengths. You could also make a chain of strengths with younger children. Write sentences on a piece of paper and your child can cut out the ones they feel are their strengths – things like:

★ I am a kind person who helps others

★ I can ask for help when I need it

★ I have a good sense of humour

★ I am a good listener

★ I am good at swimming

★ I have a good imagination

★ I can do maths problems in my head.

When they have selected which ones they feel describe them best, ask them to cut those sentence lines out and then begin making a strengths chain by looping the strips of paper into links and joining those links together. You could then display the shield or chain somewhere it can be seen and admired by the family.

Areas for reflection

1. Are you aware of your own negativity bias? Does this impact the way you interact with your children? What could you do to counter this negative focus?

2. Can you identify your own strengths? Can you identify your child's strengths? Are you providing opportunities for them to engage their strengths on a regular basis?

3. Positive feedback helps children internalise their view of the strengths they possess. How effective are you at providing positive feedback for your children about their strengths?

IN A NUTSHELL

★ The best way to help your child develop their strengths is to let them try a variety of things, even though this can be frustrating and draining when it seems like they are changing hobbies and getting involved in new activities every week.

★ Our innate negativity bias and attention on the negative has helped us survive. Turning our attention to our strengths and positive attributes helps us thrive. Shifting your focus from your child's faults and shortcomings to looking for their positive qualities and strengths not only improves your connection with them but also increases their confidence, self-efficacy and resilience.

★ When talking with children about their strengths, make sure you point out that everyone has different and unique strengths that they bring to the table. No one strength is better than another or makes kids more special than other people.

CHAPTER FIVE
Making friends

Friendship is the hardest thing in the world to explain. It's not something you learn in school. But if you haven't learned the meaning of friendship, you really haven't learned anything.

Muhammad Ali

Do you remember your first childhood friend? The one you woke up excited to see as you arrived at school inside the school gates? Delightful times playing, filled with laughter, fun and adventure. For children, forming friendships is a crucial part of growing up and a fundamental part of their social and emotional development. Even as adults, our friends remain an immensely important part of our lives, helping us cope with problems, laughing with us, sharing the good times and our proudest moments as well as being there when we simply need someone to listen and be a shoulder to lean on. Humans are innately social beings. As far back as history can trace, we have journeyed, hunted, gathered and thrived in social groups. Individuals who were alienated from their tribes frequently experienced harsh consequences.

> Friendships and social connections furnish us with an influential element of our identity and teach us skills that help us lead fulfilling lives.

As a guidance counsellor, some of the most frequent calls I had from parents were about how they could help their children manage friendship issues. One mum called me in tears one day, asking how she could help her seven-year-old son who was being excluded by his group of friends because of his new glasses. Another mum wanted to know how she could help her six-year-old daughter, who didn't seem to have any close friends in her class and wasn't invited to play at friends' houses. A dad called to ask how he could help his daughter, who had changed schools, as the kids at her new school were being incredibly mean to her when she was trying to join in. I worked alongside these families to support their kids and help them develop strategies and skills to cope with the friendship challenges they were facing. Together we built the kids' friendship skills so they could be more comfortable, confident and happy in social situations.

It's easy to assume that our children will learn to 'play nicely' with others and easily develop friendships they will keep for a lifetime. However, this is not as simple as it sounds, and things rarely go as smoothly as we would hope. Learning how to be a friend and make new friends are complex skills that require time and supportive coaching.

Disturbingly, data from around the world collated by the think tank Our World in Data, indicates that there is currently an epidemic of loneliness. The data shows:

* one-fifth of Australian, American, Canadian, British and Japanese citizens report that they feel lonely, they're not close to people or they feel left out and isolated

* one in five report that they rarely feel they have someone to talk to and turn to when they are facing problems

* one in four do not feel like they have anything in common with people around them

* 30% feel like they are not part of a close group of friends

* when compared with their less lonely colleagues, lonely individuals reported higher social anxiety and depression, poorer psychological health, fewer meaningful relationships, fewer social interactions and unhealthier quality of life.

> Having strong, enjoyable friendships is consistently, and compellingly, associated with happiness and psychological wellbeing throughout our lifespan.

Research from Dr Robert Waldinger at Harvard University has clearly demonstrated that good friends and a high level of social support is a protective factor against anxiety and depression, lowers our risk of heart disease, increases our immunity to infection and is closely related to increased levels of resilience.

A Harvard study of over 700 men that lasted for over eight decades has illustrated that positive relationships and social connection are not just good for our physical health, but they also have protective factors on our brain health. People with stronger friendships and social connections have memories that stay sharper for longer and higher levels of psychological wellbeing. Friendships and social connection are just as important for our psychological health and wellbeing as eating vegetables and getting good sleep is for our physical health and wellbeing. A lack of social connection can be more detrimental to our health than high blood pressure, smoking and obesity. Social rejection and isolation are felt in the same area of the brain where we experience physical pain.

One of the most important gifts we can give our children is the ability to connect with others and sustain those friendships. Friendship and social skills in early childhood are more predictive of outcomes in adulthood than academic skills with a significant correlation between children's social skills in kindergarten and their wellbeing at age 25. Children who displayed social competence were more likely to finish high school, go to college, find a job, and stay out of the justice system than those who exhibited lower levels of social competence.

> Just like any relationship friendships take work, and we must provide our children with the tools, strategies and skills they need to be a good friend and make and keep good friends in life.

Bullying

In today's society, bullying has become a common part of childhood. A University of Queensland study that gathered data from countries throughout the world indicated that the majority of children and teenagers had experienced some form of bullying in the past 12 months. One in three reported they had been verbally bullied, while one in seven experienced physical bullying. Up to one in ten reported experiencing a combination of both. Even the Duchess of Cambridge, Kate Middleton, was bullied at school and is now passionate about helping support children's mental health and wellbeing.

It happened to us in fifth grade. Mitchell was quite a good swimmer and had made it into a regional carnival. When he went to find his goggles before the race, they weren't in his bag. An older student had taken them and hidden them so he couldn't swim; they then magically reappeared after his races were over. He came home in tears as he missed out going to the State championships and his coach blamed him for misplacing his things. We ensured he had several pairs of goggles from then on, but these incidences kept occurring at swim meets until Mitchell decided to change sports and took up soccer. It was another sport he could do well at and helped him regain confidence and feel good about himself and his abilities.

I knew Mitchell would eventually face bullying and that this could include alliance-building, social rejection, physical aggression and damaging possessions. But I didn't think other kids would purposely steal his things to make him question himself and appear forgetful and disorganised in front of his coach.

On its Bullying No Way website, the Australian Government explains that bullying has three main features:

* ⁕ it involves a misuse of power in a relationship
* ⁕ it is ongoing and repeated
* ⁕ it involves behaviours that can cause harm.

Behaviours that do not constitute bullying include:

* ⁕ mutual arguments and disagreements (where there is no power imbalance)
* ⁕ not liking someone or a single act of social rejection

★ one-off acts of meanness or spite

★ isolated incidents of aggression, intimidation or violence.

These encounters need to be addressed and resolved but are not classified as bullying behaviours. Research by Michelle Anthony and Reyna Lindert, who wrote *Little Girls Can Be Mean: Four steps to bullyproof girls in the early grades*, has shown that before the age of eight, nastiness is largely unintentional due to young children's lack of recognition about how their actions impact on others. But after eight years of age, their cruelty becomes more intentional as, from this age, the majority of children are aware of the consequences of what they are doing.

Bullying No Way found that children who have experienced severe bullying are at a higher risk of developing significant mental health problems, anxiety, depression and suicidal ideation.

Therefore, it's important to identify if bullying is occurring and develop a plan to deal with it immediately. Warning signs of bullying can include: feeling sick, stomach-aches, headaches, unexplained injuries, loss of personal items such as books, clothes, phones, jewellery, swimmers, declining grades, not wanting to go to school, a change of sleeping or eating habits, loss of interest in doing things socially with friends, decrease in self-esteem, increase in negative self-talk and self-harm behaviours.

Many parents feel lost and unsure of how to help their children navigate this social nightmare. They fear for their child's wellbeing but feel powerless to change peer dynamics, and this often leaves them feeling helpless. One of the most common reasons parents came to see me in my role as a guidance counsellor was to ask for advice on how they could help their child handle a bullying situation at school. The good news is that there are five easy ways that parents can help their children handle bullying.

1. Listen to them, let them know that you believe them, communicate that you are sorry for what they are experiencing, and support them to problem-solve solutions when they are ready for that. Let them know you're in it together and you're going to help them figure out a way to deal with it.

2. Reinforce that reporting unkind, cruel behaviour is not snitching; telling someone about mean actions is the right thing to do, including when they witness other kids being bullied.

    Bullies function by making their victims feel powerless. By telling an adult about bullying kids can start to re-balance the power dynamic, and the bully immediately begins to lose power. Alerting an adult is not weakness, but rather a brave, powerful strategy.

3. Coach your kids about using assertive communication – simple, unemotional language that lets the bully

know that they do not intend to be a victim. Help them practise using body language that reinforces their words, such as maintaining eye contact, keeping their voice calm and even, standing up straight with shoulders back at an appropriate distance from the bully, and using the bully's name when speaking to them. These actions portray calm confidence, and a bully will detect less potential for exerting power and control. Practise role-playing different scenarios and how they could respond to a bully, so your child becomes comfortable using these skills.

4. It's also important for kids to understand that instead of observing bullying behaviour from the sidelines, they can be part of the solution. Talk to them about age-appropriate ways they could intervene to help a child who is being bullied. The best interventions have been found to be:

- **Partnering with the victim to remove them from danger** – Physically standing with the victim if it's physically safe, turning them away from the bully and walking in the direction of adult help while saying something like, "I've been looking for you" or "You look upset" or "The teacher wanted me to find you."

- **Get help** – Enlist other kids' support for the victim by calling them over, saying, "We need your help." The group can then confront the bully by saying, "Stop being mean," and encourage the victim to walk away with them, "C'mon, let's go!"

5. Alert the school to the problem and find a teacher, guidance counsellor or administrator who both you and your child feel comfortable talking with – this will be at separate times but shows your child that you trust that person to help. Schools take bullying very seriously and want to work with families to address issues.

Friendships can bring joy and positivity into our children's lives and is one of the things that will sustain them in times of hardship. Learning how to grow strong friendships is an important life skill.

When problems occur

Friendships are full of ups and downs and along with the fun, adventures, laughter and good times sometimes your children may fall out with a friend and this can occasionally cause hurt feelings, sadness, conflict and anger. If your child has fallen out with a friend, make time to talk with them about what happened, how they feel and how their friend might be feeling. Listen to their concerns and acknowledge their feelings before offering any ideas about solutions. Explain that it's normal for friends to get on each other's nerves sometimes and that feelings of frustration and irritation are different from truly not liking each other anymore. Remind them that there are always ups and downs in friendships and that they can leave a group of friends if they feel uncomfortable or don't like what they are doing. Offer some ideas about the next steps they could take and follow up with them the next day when they come home from school to see how it all worked out.

1. TEACH SOCIAL SKILLS

As parents we need to help our kids understand the importance of greeting people in a pleasant way, talking to others politely, taking turns, sharing, listening to others and taking someone else's feelings into account. These skills can be supported and developed by arranging plenty of opportunities for your child to meet a variety of different people. Social skills can also be practised by role-playing with your children, so they can try their skills out in a familiar environment with a safe and supportive person until they become more proficient.

2. MODEL HOW FRIENDSHIPS WORK

Our children watch everything we do, which is a wonderful way for them to learn about friendships. Let them observe how you behave with your friends, how you surround yourself with people who support, encourage and treat you well. Let them see you investing time and energy into your friendships and explain that no one is born knowing how to make friends. Let them know that we all need to learn how to do it and that everyone can become better at it, just like we can learn how to read and become better at that too. Model friendship behaviours you want them to learn – sharing, turn-taking, listening, laughing, negotiating, taking other's feelings into account and problem-solving. That way, they can observe them in action and begin to understand how they work.

3. FRIENDS DO THE FIVE

We need to explicitly describe the qualities that make a good friend so that our children will understand how to be a good friend, as well as how to tell if another person is being a good friend to them. Explain that being a good friend means being kind, a good listener, honest, unselfish and trustworthy. An easy way to help your child remember the characteristics of what makes a good friend is to draw an outline around their hand. In the palm write **Friends do the Five**, then write these five things – one on each finger; Be kind, Be a good listener, Tell the truth, Take turns and share, Keep promises. When you've practised this activity they have a tool they can use anywhere to evaluate if someone is being a good friend.

Encourage your child to also think about their friend's feelings and consider how their actions may impact on their friend. Describe how good friends show an interest in the other person and want to know what they are interested in, and that they do this by asking questions and listening. Let them know that another trait of being a good friend is that they are both a good winner and loser – that things do not have to go their way all the time. You can also discuss what bad friends might do such as: being selfish, not listening, not sharing, making fun of other people, ignoring them, snatching or taking things that they want, being dishonest or being unkind. This encourages them not to tolerate those behaviours from others as well as reflect on their own behaviour and not to do those things with their friends.

4. MODEL HOW TO PROBLEM-SOLVE

When our children experience challenges with siblings or friends, it's easy for us to intervene and make everything right again. However, it's better to involve them in the problem-solving process as it provides them with skills they will use for the rest of their life. Encourage them to be part of the problem-solving process by asking them to describe what they think is happening, suggest possible solutions and then test one out. Be there to scaffold the process, supporting them through it and helping them reflect on how their solution is going by asking, "How did that work out?" This encourages them to reflect on the action they took, evaluate if it was successful and provides a safe environment for them to try new things and ideas.

5. TRAFFIC LIGHTS STRATEGY

Friendships are not always smooth sailing; children will have disagreements and arguments, and we need to help them develop skills to resolve these in productive ways. Assure your child that it is okay to have disagreements as long as they don't hurt the other person. Talk with them about ways they can resolve their differences and how to make up after a disagreement or argument. It may be that they need to acknowledge that their behaviour caused the problem, own their mistake and apologise to their friend so they can move forward.

You can also help them develop strategies and phrases they can use if they believe their friend has caused the problem like, "I felt angry when you wrecked my Lego creation." One activity that can help scaffold children's conflict resolution skills is thinking of a traffic light. When a conflict or problem has occurred ask your child to close their eyes, think of a red traffic light, take four deep breaths and think of something they find calming. Then when their traffic light turns yellow, they think of two ways they can handle the situation. When their traffic light turns green, they choose a way to resolve the conflict (ask for help, go outside to calm down, tell their friend how they feel) and try that strategy out.

Areas for reflection

1. How good is your child at making friends? Have they learned how to share, take turns, and notice other's feelings?

2. What do you think your child most needs to learn about being a friend?

3. Stop and think back to your childhood. Were you bullied as a child? How did you respond to those incidents, and do they still impact you today? Is this affecting how you talk to your child about bullying?

IN A NUTSHELL

★ There is a large amount of scientific evidence that our social relationships are a key to mental health and wellbeing. Having good friends is continually and strongly correlated with positive life outcomes.

★ Friendship skills are not innate, and we need to explicitly teach our children the skills to be a good friend. We also need to provide them with knowledge so they can identify when someone is not being such a good friend to them.

★ Friendships are full of ups and downs that are a normal part of growing up. Bullying is not, and can have a significant impact on your child's mental health. If you suspect your child is being bullied, it's important to develop a plan to deal with it immediately.

CHAPTER SIX
Encouraging kindness and empathy

Connection is why we're here. We are hardwired to connect with others, it's what gives purpose and meaning to our lives, and without it, there is suffering.

Brené Brown

Growing up, my parents instilled a strong sense of empathy in me. Our family frequently volunteered at church events, community days and bake sales for charities. Donating my time to help others was just something I saw as a natural thing to do. One of my favourite activities was decorating shirts with Hobbytex fabric paint and donating them to the children's hospital. I can still remember the smiles on the kids' faces and the buzz I got out of being able to make someone's day a little brighter.

This empathy continued to show up throughout my school-
ing and was the main reason I was bullied. I then slipped
into mild depression when I was 16. Until then, I'd never had
any trouble at school; I got along with most people but had
strong empathy for those kids who were a little different and
isolated.

One day I saw a group of kids I was friends with bullying
another young man who had significant learning difficulties. They'd taken his hat, were throwing it to one another,
laughing and taunting him. Something just snapped inside
me – I knew this was nasty, wrong and had to end. I stepped
in and told them they needed to stop it and give his hat back.
They looked at me like I had two heads and kept throwing
it, laughing as they did. I reiterated the fact that they needed
to stop it, then caught the hat and gave it back to its owner.

From that point on the bullying and social isolation started. It
was subtle at first but then became more exclusionary, alien-
ating me from all my friends. I could cope with the teasing
and physical aspects of the bullying; it was the social isolation
that hurt the most. Each day when I caught the bus home,
tears would sting in my eyes, but I was determined not to
let them beat me. Instead, I went to the library at lunchtime,
helped teachers out and finally found some other kids who
didn't fit in. I spent the final two years of high school hanging
out with them.

In his book, *Social,* Matthew Lieberman describes research which used functional magnetic resonance imaging (fMRI) machines to capture images of our brains responding to stimuli. It revealed that we are deeply social beings and that when we experience rejection or other types of social pain, our brains hurt in similar ways to when we experience physical pain. This need for connection and belonging has also been highlighted by Brené Brown in her work when she explained: 'A deep sense of love and belonging is an irresistible need of all people. We are biologically, cognitively, physically and spiritually wired to love, to be loved and to belong. When those needs are not met, we don't function as we were meant to. We break. We fall apart. We numb. We ache.'

> Just like we have a fundamental need for food and shelter, we also have a fundamental need to belong to a group, feel connected, and know that we are making a difference in our world.

We yearn to feel valued, supported and needed by others. A sense of belonging, meaning, and purpose is associated with increased psychological wellbeing and resilience, whereas a sense of isolation and a feeling of not belonging increases the risk of both psychological and physical disorders.

Our sense of meaning and purpose comes from a feeling of connection with something bigger than ourselves – that we're contributing to others, or society, in a bigger way. It's outward-focused rather than inward-focused on our own goals and pursuits. Having a sense of meaning and purpose in life improves both mental and physical health, increases optimism, enhances resiliency and self-esteem, enables better adaptation when people face setbacks and decreases the chances of depression, which makes them essential elements of mental fitness.

As adults, we may have already found our own sense of meaning and purpose, but we cannot simply pass this on to our children. They need to uncover their meaning and purpose for themselves. Alex Korb, a neuroscientist, explains that young children can't comprehend notions such as meaning and purpose. But they can relate to what matters to them, what is important to them, what interests them and what they care about.

Kindness, compassion and empathy

Korb also examines how kindness, compassion and empathy towards others facilitates the discovery of meaning and purpose. Kindness is the quality of being friendly, generous and considerate of others without expecting anything in return. Compassion is the awareness of others' distress and the desire to help alleviate that distress, and empathy is the ability to sense, identify and understand other people's emotions. Korb explains that as well as improving our health and strengthening our social bonds, kindness, compassion and empathy are also an antidote to depression.

When I was ten, we moved from Brisbane, Australia, to live in Oregon, USA, for a year. This meant going to a new school in a new city and making new friends. Due to the differences in school years, I started in the middle of the year and felt very out of place. I was the new kid in town who didn't know anyone and had a funny accent. I vividly remember sitting down with a group of girls during the first lunch break. The discomfort was palpable, I didn't realise I wasn't supposed to sit with them, but their body language soon let me know. I shuffled away and felt hot tears sting in my eyes. It was then that another girl came up to me and said, "Hi, you're new, aren't you? Come sit with us." She demonstrated empathy and kindness which I have never forgotten. We are still good friends, even though we live half a world apart, and that one act of kindness influenced both how I have parented and taught.

In *Social* Matthew Lieberman explains that children and young people do not simply learn kindness by thinking and talking about it; it is best learned when they experience it.

> When our kids feel kindness from one another, they then understand what it feels like and can reproduce that feeling.

He also found that the seeds of kindness, compassion and empathy exist even when we are infants and that they are skills that can be taught. However, for these seeds to fully bloom, we need to nurture them.

Anna, one of the mums I worked with when I was a guidance counsellor, came to see me because she was worried about her son Jimmy. Jimmy was five years old, and they were at the park with a group of other kids from school. Anna was watching Jimmy and his friends playing and noticed that several kids were teasing Matthew, who was one of Jimmy's best friends, and Matthew started crying. She was concerned because she had expected Jimmy to go straight over to Matthew and comfort him, but Jimmy didn't. She was worried that Jimmy didn't understand Matthew's feelings and wasn't going to grow up to be kind.

I reassured her that Jimmy was not going to grow up into an unkind person who lacked empathy and suggested she gently talk about the situation with Jimmy when there was a calm time at home to understand his version of what he was thinking and feeling. Anna came back to see me after she had talked to Jimmy and explained that he had been worried that those kids would be mean to him, too, if he tried to help Jimmy because that had happened before in the playground. Anna had then spoken with Jimmy and problem-solved different ways of handling the situation if it occurred again, as well as letting him know how proud she was of him for being kind and caring enough to notice that Matthew was upset and for having the courage to have helped Matthew previously.

When I was alerted to what had been going on in the playground at school, I was able to implement a program for the kindergartners and pre-schoolers that encouraged kindness, empathy and compassion.

Amid growing concerns about the epidemic of bullying in our schools, parents and educators frequently ask me how they can put an end to both bullying in schools and within their communities. I explain that the most crucial thing they can do is demonstrate kindness, compassion and empathy for their children. It is these small acts, which may seem insignificant to us, that are surprisingly powerful in fostering concern and care for others.

> Nurturing compassion in children and young people is one of the most important ways to stop emotional, verbal and physical aggression from developing.

Empathy does not usually fully develop until the age of eight, so younger children will have a hard time sharing and understanding other people's feelings. However experts such as Korb and Lieberman have found that there is a critical period between the ages of four and seven, when children's brains are very receptive to developing lasting habits of kindness and compassion. Simply hoping that our children will grow up to be kind people who have empathy for others is not enough – we need to help them develop these skills by consciously teaching them kindness.

Self-compassion

Self-compassion is another important skill we need to nurture in our kids. As a guidance counsellor, I frequently worked with kids who were incredibly hard and critical of themselves. One such student was Michelle, who was in the sixth grade. Michelle was in foster care and had just started at our school after attending three previous schools that year. She was entering her classroom, and the deputy principal was there greeting everyone as they came in. Michelle accidentally dropped her water bottle and books onto the deputy principal's foot. The deputy exclaimed, "Oww!" but wasn't angry and didn't reprimand Michelle in any way. Michelle felt very embarrassed, mumbled sorry as she quickly picked up her belongings, and then moved to the back of the room. Michelle shared this story with me when she came to check in at lunchtime, saying, "I'm just so clumsy and stupid." I asked if the deputy had been upset and she said, "I don't think so, they didn't yell or swear at me, so I guess no they weren't, but I still think I'm a loser." I explained that sometimes accidents happen, and that the deputy would have understood that.

Michelle was holding herself to unrealistic expectations and felt like an absolute failure when she didn't meet those expectations or got something wrong in her own opinion. I worked with her to begin developing self-compassion so that she could instead view herself as a beautiful human being who doesn't always get things perfectly right, and that is okay.

Self-compassion is when we accept who we are and believe that we are worthy of love and respect, both during good and bad times. Self-compassion enables young people to be kind to themselves when they make a mistake instead of feeling ashamed or guilty. It guards young people against believing that when they fail, it's because they are hopelessly flawed and have nothing positive to contribute or live for.

1. MODEL IT

Imagine telling your four-year-old why they should give their unused toys to an unknown charity. Your child would be thinking, "Wait. You want me to do what?" Their brains don't work that way, particularly when they're very young. Instead, visualise how you live on a day-to-day basis. If you're kind to people, generous, polite, give of your time, collect canned goods for the local food bank, donate clothes and other goods to charities or visit elderly neighbours who may be lonely, your children will learn to do the same. Our kids are sponges and internalise what we as parents do, more than what we say.

If we suggest they could donate some of their toys, we also need to be mindful that they may have a connection to certain toys that we don't understand. Let them choose which ones they want to donate, as this gives them a sense of control and autonomy.

2. BE INTENTIONAL

We can't just assume our children will become generous people who want to help others. Not only do we need to model these behaviours, but we can also intentionally point out the acts of generosity, kindness and contribution we witness or experience throughout the day so our kids can start to understand how to integrate it into their own lives.

For example, you could have a conversation at bedtime that goes something like this, "Let's think about all the helpers we saw today and how they helped people." This is particularly appropriate when there is a lot of terrible news such as bushfires which can be overwhelming for children. With older kids, you could talk with them about one person they helped, or one person that made a difference in their life that day. Intentionally focus on the positive aspects of the world, so children can see that everybody can make a difference. The news is frequently full of gloom, but you can intentionally focus on amazing articles and stories that demonstrate kindness, empathy, service and contribution and share these with your kids. This is not about ignoring reality; it is about supporting our children's impressionable minds to develop an optimistic and hopeful outlook and disposition.

3. VOLUNTEER WITH YOUR KIDS

Talk with your kids and identify ways they might like to volunteer to help people – it could be helping to clean up a local park, helping out at a dog shelter, walking in a fun run to raise money for charity, visiting an old people's home or going with you to help out at a soup kitchen or food pantry. When they are helping people less advantaged than themselves, it brings home how blessed they truly are and reinforces a sense of gratitude.

4. DONATE TO A CHARITY OR NON-PROFIT ORGANISATION

In our family, we make it a habit once a year to go through all of our things and set aside toys, clothing, sporting goods and anything else that's in good condition that we don't use anymore. We also go to the store and select toys or other gifts for families less fortunate at Christmas time. We then make a time to deliver the items to a deserving charity or non-profit organisation together. They are always grateful for basic necessities, food and gifts to give to those in need. Organisations like Global Giving or Givit are also great ways of making a difference and starting a conversation with your kids.

5. PROVIDE OPPORTUNITIES TO PRACTISE EMPATHY

Children need to have regular opportunities to consider other people's feelings, circumstances and perspectives. From this, regularly practising empathy and kindness become a natural habit for them. Ask your kids about their classmates and friends, and help them take a different perspective than their own. Discuss with them what it would be like for them if someone picked on them or teased them – helping them articulate these feelings will better enable them to understand how others might feel in those circumstances.

This discussion can also be accompanied by an activity that I used with both my Mitchell and the students in my classrooms. I asked the kids to take an apple, say something nasty and then drop the apple on the floor. This occurred several times – after which I cut the apple open and showed them that even though they couldn't see the hurt their words had caused on the outside, there was still damage on the inside.

Areas for reflection

1. Are you consciously teaching your children kindness? Most parents hope that their children are kind to others, but few explicitly teach their kids about kindness and empathy. How are your children learning about kindness?

2. In what ways have you helped or given to others in the past few weeks? When was the last time you did a random act of kindness? What reaction or impact did your kindness and generosity have on the other person?

3. What motivates you to help others?

IN A NUTSHELL

★ Being kind to others improves our psychological wellbeing and builds our mental fitness resources. Experiencing kindness and empathy increases the likelihood of showing kindness to others and having more empathy for other's perspectives and feelings.

★ One of the most effective ways of tackling bullying is nurturing compassion in children and young people as this can help stop emotional, verbal and physical aggression from developing.

★ Teaching our children self-compassion is also very important as being kind and gentle with themselves combats their harsh self-criticism and negative self-talk and increases their resilience and ability to manage challenging situations.

CHAPTER SEVEN
Fostering gratitude

Just an observation: it is impossible to be both grateful and depressed. Those with a grateful mindset tend to see the message in the mess. And even though life may knock them down, the grateful find reasons, if even small ones, to get up.

Steve Maraboli

When my favourite aunt first met Mitchell, then aged five, she warmly hugged him and gave him a toy she'd brought all the way from Europe. Mitchell wouldn't even look at it; let alone say, "Thank you." I was absolutely mortified and a little concerned that we were raising an entitled brat. One of the most consistent worries that I heard from both parents and teachers when I was a guidance counsellor was that this generation of children can sometimes be cynical, entitled, egocentric beings who seem to be amazingly ungrateful for all that is done for them. You may have seen it or felt it yourself (maybe even within your own family). We've all met kids who feel entitled to have everything their way and expect things to be provided for them on a silver platter without rolling up their sleeves and putting in any effort. This can be incredibly frustrating for parents who are trying to raise happy, healthy kids and give them every opportunity they can, and yet feel like their kids aren't thankful for the things they are given.

With the overwhelming abundance of opportunities, material possessions and privileges the majority of kids in the Western World enjoy, it is not hard to see why so many of them end up feeling entitled.

When children are used to getting things through no effort of their own and feel entitled to be the boss all the time, it is much more likely that they will feel extremely disillusioned when they don't get what they want and will be unable to manage when things don't go their way.

I am sure we have all witnessed what happens at birthday parties these days where games like pass the parcel have been changed, so no one loses, and everyone wins a prize. This excessive sense of entitlement is creating significant mental health problems for our kids and decreasing their levels of resilience.

Developing a sense of gratitude emphasises the fact that all those toys, belongings, opportunities and creature comforts don't just magically appear out of thin air. When children pause to recognise and appreciate that the things they are given and the opportunities they are presented with have been given to them by someone else, this facilitates an understanding of how interconnected we all are.

According to Professor Robert Emmons, who has studied gratitude for over three decades, gratitude has two components – the first is noticing and actively appreciating good things in the world, like the gifts, benefits and opportunities we have received. The second component is recognising that the source of these good things is outside ourselves – we acknowledge that other people, or even a higher power if you have a faith belief and mindset, have given us numerous gifts both big and small that contribute to the richness of our lives.

> This doesn't mean that grateful people don't have day-to-day hassles and problems; it simply means that they focus on the good stuff in their lives.

This positive focus balances out our brain's natural tendency to focus on what's wrong and what we are lacking. This is our brain's way of keeping us safe, but when we focus on all the negatives in our lives, we create a mindset of lack and limitation which has substantial implications for our psychological wellbeing and mental health.

James was a ten-year-old boy who attended school in a wealthy suburb but had a very different living situation to his peers. He and his mum lived in a long-term women's refuge due to domestic violence and financial hardships which meant he had to walk to school and would often not have the equipment or books he needed. As the guidance counsellor, I'd regularly check in to see how James was going. One day I saw he had new books and a different school bag. James proudly told me, with a huge smile on his face, that his teacher had given them to him and expressed how thankful he was for her kindness, saying, "Mrs Ryan is so lovely, she gave me this stuff cause she knows I didn't have the right books. And look at the bag she found for me, isn't it great? I really appreciate her giving me these things, and I drew her this picture to tell her thank you." Other children may have felt jealous, angry, resentful or embarrassed because they didn't have the right books, clothes, a nice bag or a house of their own to live in, but not James. His mother had helped him develop a deep sense of gratitude for the things many of us take for granted like having a safe place to live, food to eat, family, friends at school, his caring teachers, even basic access to a computer and the internet in the refuge's common room, and this had a significant impact on his approach to life. James also wrote a letter to the principal, letting her know how much he appreciated Mrs Ryan's kindness and generosity. He wanted to let everyone know how special she was, what kind things she did for her students, and how grateful he was to have her as his teacher. His positivity was infectious and rubbed off on anyone his life touched.

Over 25 years of research by Emmons has shown that consistently practising gratitude is associated with higher psychological wellbeing and a range of other positive benefits such as reduced levels of depression, stronger social bonds and friendships, less loneliness, lower stress levels, a stronger immune system, better sleep, being more generous, kind and compassionate, increased resilience and being less likely to take drugs.

> Gratitude, and having a grateful disposition, is something that can be learned and developed throughout life.

As parents, we need to consciously create situations, routines and habits that cultivate gratitude in our children, so that it becomes a regular part of their daily lives. I'm not asking you to force a sense of gratitude on them by saying things like, "Think about all the children living in poorer countries who don't have rooms like yours or food on their plates." This might cause them to feel guilty and resentful, not genuinely grateful for what they have. We don't want to create a situation where they are simply mouthing platitudes of gratitude without truly feeling the underlying emotion. Instead, we want to give our kids the opportunity to develop their own sense of genuine gratitude and thankfulness for all the good in their lives.

There are a lot of ways we can foster gratitude and appreciation in our children. I'd like to take this opportunity to thank Professor Emmons and all the other researchers who have spent their careers exploring the benefits of gratitude as well as the parents who have shared their ideas, both with me personally as well as on their blogs.

Model gratitude

Our kids want to be like us. The example we set, especially when they are little, becomes indelibly etched in their minds. We provide a model for what to say and do in different situations and contexts. When we express our gratitude in words, by writing notes or letters or through acts of reciprocity, these all teach children how to be grateful. Doing this is a way to explicitly illustrate your appreciation for all the good things in your life and shows your kids that being thankful is an attitude that is valued by you. We can also express gratitude for the things our kids do by saying things like, "Thanks for helping clear the table after dinner, I appreciate it" or "I appreciate the way you played so nicely with your sister, even after she knocked down your castle" or "Your room looks so tidy with all your toys put away in the basket, I appreciate you remembering to pack up." These conversations reinforce them for behaving kindly, convey that you've paid attention to the effort they've made and also model how to verbally show appreciation.

We also need to be conscious of modelling that the size of the good fortune doesn't matter. We show gratitude for a large gift but also smaller simple things like a delicious cup of coffee, a beautiful flower, a lovely drawing or piece of art or a sunny day.

As adults, there are times and days when it's harder for us to feel grateful for the things in our lives, and this is the same for our kids.

> I'm not suggesting we create robots who only see the good in everything. It's about fostering a sense of gratitude and modelling the fact that things may sometimes not go the way we want them to, but there are ways we can look at the situation to be grateful for the learning we took away and there are good things that can come out of something unpleasant that occurred.

For example, you could ask your nine-year-old to consider not being in the same class with all their friends in a new school year as an opportunity to make new friends or ask your teenager to consider the possibility that if someone breaks up with them, it may be creating an opening for an even better relationship.

1. INSTIL MANNERS

When we model the use of polite manners, saying please and thank you for things, this shows our children that we don't believe we are simply entitled to everything we want, but in fact, appreciate all the good things that come into our lives. When 'thank you' is instilled in children's vocabulary at home when they are young, it becomes a lifelong habit. Even if, like Mitchell with my aunt, they don't say 'thank you' at first, you can gently restate a sentence with 'thank you' inserted or suggest saying 'thank you' together. One thing to remember is that kids under seven have difficulty understanding others' feelings and being internally motivated to do the right thing and say thank you. However, we can actively instil a sense of gratitude through modelling. As they become a little older, talk to your children about generosity and the meaning of giving. Explain why they should be thankful and prompt them to consider the thought behind the gift they were given and what the act of giving meant to the person who gave them the gift.

2. ENCOURAGE CHILDREN TO NOTICE AND THANK OTHERS

Spend time helping your child to recognise good things that have happened to them and steer them towards developing an appreciation for those people who purposefully helped them, were kind or did good things for them. For example, you may have learned through your conversation with your child that one of their friends got off the swing in a crowded playground so your child could have a turn. You could use this opportunity to suggest your child appreciate that their friend got off the swing even though they didn't have to so that your child could have a turn. Encourage your child to acknowledge these good events and say thank you. We can also set a powerful example for our children by acknowledging and thanking people who quietly serve us in any way from a barista serving our coffee, the bus driver, a cleaner in the toilets at the local mall, or people who have served in the military, especially on ANZAC Day or Veterans Day.

3. PLAY 'HOW WOULD YOU FEEL WITHOUT IT?'

This game can be played anywhere and at any time. Simply choose an item and ask your child what they would feel like without that item in their lives, for example, the family car, their play station, the refrigerator, their bike. This game gently prompts children to develop gratitude for many items they simply consider it 'normal' to have and therefore take for granted.

4. CREATE A GRATITUDE JAR OR BOX

This is an adapted version of keeping a gratitude journal. A family may decide to have a beautiful box or jar in the kitchen or in another central part of the house. Place brightly coloured sticky notes and pens next to the jar or box and whenever family members are feeling grateful for someone or something, they write it on a sticky note and add it to the jar or box. Then the family can choose when to read them out together – this could be done every week, every month or at the end of the year to celebrate all the good that has happened throughout the year.

5. FAMILY RITUALS

Many families have rituals acknowledging the things they are grateful for – this could be done at the dinner table each night. You could go around the table and ask each member to name one or two things they're grateful for – this can also be a good conversation starter. Other families take the time to recognise and appreciate all the people that helped contribute to putting the food on their table. Another ritual that I did with Mitchell for years was to read a story before bed, and then I'd invite him to tell me some of the things he was thankful for during the day. They could be things that went well or felt good – they didn't have to be huge. It could be as simple as seeing his favourite friend, watching a dog at the park on the way home, swimming well in a race (even if he didn't win) or finishing a difficult set of math problems and feeling proud he kept at it. This helped him focus on the positive before he went to sleep.

Areas for reflection

1. Did you grow up in a grateful household? How has that impacted your outlook on life? Are your children growing up in a household where gratitude is encouraged?

2. Are you a role model of thanking and giving for your children? Expressing thanks and generosity are two essential components of a grateful mindset.

3. What are three ways you could help your child develop a more grateful mindset in the coming month?

IN A NUTSHELL

★   Robert Emmons' research for the past 30 years has identified that having an attitude of gratitude significantly contributes to our positive mental health and wellbeing.

★   Gratitude encourages us to notice and focus on all the good things we have in our lives and be thankful for it and where it came from, rather than constantly thinking about what we don't have.

★   It's not difficult to practise gratitude, but it does require commitment. This is both a psychological commitment to focus on all the good in your life, as well as a time commitment to make it a habit. That's why it's great to start a family gratitude ritual or routine, which is an expected part of the day, where you all practise grateful thinking.

CHAPTER EIGHT
Learning to fail

Do not judge me by my successes; judge me by how many times I fell down and got back up again.

Nelson Mandela

One day I visited a grade three classroom to see how the students had settled in and if there were any that would require extra support. I observed the students during their writing time, and one little girl had written two and a half pages already. A little boy saw me watching the little girl and said, "She's writing a great story, miss – she's the clever one in our class, she always writes long stories, and they're so good." He didn't do this in an envious way, he seemed to be proud of his classmate and eager for me to find out how well she could write. When I explained that I was sure they would all write good stories because I could see how hard they were working, he again reiterated that his classmate would have the top story because she was cleverest in the class at writing. What I had just observed in that classroom was a classic example of a fixed mindset. That eight-year-old little boy thought that his classmate was the 'clever one' and that no matter how hard he, or the other kids in the class tried or how much effort they put in, that little girl was always going to be the 'clever' one with the 'best' stories.

As humans, we all talk to ourselves – whether we realise it or not. We all have an inner voice that I like to call the 'itty bitty crappy committee'. It's the voice in our mind that says things we usually do not say out loud. This inner dialogue frequently occurs without us even realising it's happening and runs as a subtle commentary in the background of everything we do. On average, we have anywhere between 40,000–60,000 thoughts per day – of those, approximately 60 per cent are negative and 85 per cent are repetitive thoughts. We need to teach children how to talk to themselves in a positive, kind and reassuring way and reframe negative thoughts so they can think more realistically.

Research undertaken by Professor Carol Dweck at Stanford University has revealed that a parent's beliefs or mindset about what makes a person successful can significantly impact how successful our kids will be academically and socially, as well as their future level of achievement and income as adults and contribute to the mind-set they individually develop about learning, effort and persistence.

Attitudes to learning matter, and Professor Dweck identified two distinct mindsets – a *'fixed mindset'*, where people believe that talents, abilities and intelligence are fixed inborn traits that cannot be changed. For example, we're either good at maths or not, smart or dumb and sporty or not. When people with a fixed mindset face a setback, they often make excuses and apportion blame on other people or circumstances. Their sense of identity and self-worth is so intertwined with their success or failure that they cultivate a fear of failing and become averse to taking risks.

> People with a growth mindset believe that we can all change, learn and grow and that success comes as a result of effort, perseverance, the willingness to try a repertoire of different approaches and strategies, and the resilience to bounce back after making mistakes, not getting things right or failing on your first attempt.

David Yeager, Carol Dweck and several colleagues investigated young people's mindsets and found that those with a fixed mindset reported higher levels of stress, poorer physical health and lower grades. Young people with a growth mindset reported being less stressed and anxious, had better physical health, better grades, had less depression and better relationships. They also strengthened our understanding that children, adolescents and adults are capable of developing a growth mindset. Having a growth or fixed mindset is not an individual trait that is stable for life, our mindset may vary depending on what we are doing, and most people are somewhere in between the two.

Through my experience as a guidance counsellor many parents describe their children's abilities in fixed-mindset ways – "she inherited her dad's talent for maths, she's just brilliant with numbers" or "he draws so well, I know he's going to be an artist for sure." When we praise our children in these ways, we encourage them to view their talents and skills as inborn, which devalues the role of effort and perseverance in learning and achievement.

A child's mindset and the expectations they have about their abilities have considerable influence on their willingness to try new things, take risks and learn from their mistakes.

> Children's internalised beliefs about their abilities affect their self-talk and become self-fulfilling prophecies that confirm their expectations and beliefs about their abilities.

If they believe that their intelligence, creative talents, athletic skill or anything else that they are good at is innate, rather than believing that these skills and talents can be developed through practise and effort, they are less likely to stick with tasks when they become hard or try new ways of doing things.

Somehow in our culture, we have developed the belief that protecting our kids from discomfort and the pain of disappointment is the way to be effective parents. There is a misconception that if children suffer any discomfort growing up, there's something you're doing wrong as a parent. Although it can be tempting to help a child whenever they're struggling, rescuing them from distress will reinforce to them that they're helpless.

One of my best friends had a 13-year-old son who was very good academically. He received A grades all throughout his primary school education and did not have to study a great deal; in fact, he spent much of it socialising and playing sport. He was particularly talented at French and seemed naturally gifted at learning languages. When he went to high school, he encountered other students who had been studying French longer than he had and recognised that he wouldn't be eliciting the same sort of praise from his teachers or parents if he didn't do as well and receive the best grade in the class. He started making excuses about wanting to drop French to concentrate on his other subjects, about not having enough time to fit everything in and about how he wasn't enjoying it as much as he used to. It became very clear that he was operating from a fixed-mindset approach. My friend was considering speaking to the school about allowing him to change subjects mid-semester. I spoke with her about this and encouraged her to support him continuing French for at least the rest of the year. If she had enabled him to switch out of French because he didn't want to look bad or feel uncomfortable, she would have reinforced his fixed mindset about his talents and skills. She would also have supported his desire to give up quickly because he was afraid to fail and look less than perfect. Instead she started using growth mindset encouragement and praise such as, "Some of the other kids may be better at French than you, but that's okay as all that matters is that you try your hardest and enjoy French because you love it so much."

> Kids need to build up a tolerance for discomfort, an emotional callous if you will. Building this tolerance for discomfort is important because discomfort is a big part of life.

We all have to learn to sit in traffic, to lose a game or to be passed over for a promotion. Life is naturally full of failures, even for the most successful people. Teach your kids healthy coping strategies to deal with discomfort, and coach them as they practise. With your support, they can learn that uncomfortable emotions are tolerable.

> Embracing a growth mindset permits parents and kids to reframe mistakes as learning opportunities and believe that they can improve with effort and perseverance – they may not be perfect, but they can always find ways to develop their skills and grow.

Learning from our setbacks, mistakes and failures, developing the perseverance and grit to keep going and having the resilience to try again if something hasn't worked are all attributes we want to instil in our kids.

Angela Duckworth has found that some kids innately have more grit than others, but there are a multitude of things we can do as parents to help our children develop their grit and perseverance. When you've observed your child sticking at a task point it out, let them know you noticed and are proud of them. Help them focus on the little steps that lead to successfully achieving their goal or overcoming an obstacle. Phrases such as, "I can see you're working really hard on that…" help your child see the benefit in the process, rather than just focusing on the reward at the end. If we model persistence and determination when we are faced with tough challenges, they will see what it looks like in real life.

Having the opportunity to try new things and make mistakes that they learn from shows kids that they can overcome challenges they may face in the future. This encourages them to develop an optimistic mindset and feel hopeful about the future. There is one important caveat, though, and that is to make sure the challenges your kids face are developmentally appropriate, as too difficult a challenge can cause them to feel anxious and fear failure.

It's important to talk with our children about how failing is a natural opportunity to learn that helps them identify what they can't do, or don't know, yet. If things have not gone so well, always acknowledge what they did well before you talk with them about what they could do differently next time. Encourage them to reflect on what happened and ask themselves the following questions: "What went well? What would I change if I could?" Work with them to identify how they can develop a plan of action to influence events in the future, as this will give them the confidence to try again.

Allowing our kids to make mistakes and feel discomfort can feel very uncomfortable. Watching our children make mistakes is painful – whether they're falling out with friends or off a jungle gym, our instinct is to protect them. It's hard to watch them feel uncomfortable and upset. Yet they learn important lessons from making mistakes and gain confidence when they bounce back from them. We need to teach our children that mistakes are part of the learning process, so they don't feel ashamed or embarrassed about getting something wrong. When they're allowed to struggle and sometimes fail, we allow them to develop important social and emotional skills. Trying something and making a mistake or failing is part of growing and learning. Children who don't develop healthy coping strategies when they make a mistake or fail are much more vulnerable to developing anxiety. Of course, we don't risk their safety or refuse to respond when what is needed most is reassurance. However, our role should be to support and guide, not fix everything for them.

1. INTRODUCE THE TWO MINDSETS

Teach the basic differences of growth and fixed mindsets explaining it in language that kids can understand. For example, a growth mindset is when we know that our brain can become better at something and stronger with practice and that when we try things that are hard and don't give up, we're building our brains just like we can build our muscles. Whereas when we have a fixed mindset, we don't think we can become better at things or that our brains can change and grow. People with fixed mindsets want to give up and quit when things become hard because they believe that they're not good at it and never will be. It can also cause people who believe they are already 'good' at something to plateau and not improve their skills or capabilities.

Even the four and five-year-olds I worked with could differentiate between the different mindsets of storybook characters after several lessons about the basic differences between fixed and growth mindsets. I would also frequently hear the grade five and six students I worked with point out fixed mindsets in each other.

2. CHALLENGE NEGATIVE THOUGHTS

We can teach kids to identify and challenge negative thoughts that undermine their belief in their ability to successfully master a task. We have to help them identify their negative self-talk thoughts and can do this by listening for when we hear them say things about themselves that are negative, things that begin with 'I can't', 'I never' or 'I always'. Talk with them about how they feel when they hear themselves say these things and point out how that can stop them from doing their best because it takes away their confidence. Then provide them with evidence to prove why their negative thoughts are inaccurate and help them swap the negative thoughts with a positive, more helpful concept.

3. DEMONSTRATE NEURONS GETTING STRONGER

You will need a ball of string or wool for this activity. The activity demonstrates how each time we practise something our neural connections become stronger. You hold the ball of wool and explain to your child that the first time we do anything there are weak connections between the neurons in our brain because we are just learning that skill. Then pass the ball of wool to them and say, "This is the first connection between our neurons when we are learning something new, as you can see it's not very strong." Then explain that the connections get stronger as we practise that skill and demonstrate this by passing the ball of wool backwards and forwards between you and your child. Once you have at least eight strands of wool going between the two of you, gather all of them together and show your child how strong the connection is now. Then help them come up with a list of activities they once found difficult but became easier after they practised, such as brushing their teeth, riding a bike, skating, swimming, solving math problems. Celebrate their amazing brain for making strong connections as they learnt each skill.

4. ALLOW KIDS TO BE FRUSTRATED AND UNCOMFORTABLE

We need to allow our kids to feel frustrated and uncomfortable when they are pushing through tasks that require effort. We need to help them learn how to deal with these feelings, take a breath, redirect themselves, challenge their negative thoughts, try something different and then eventually overcome their frustration because they stuck at it and worked it out. If we shield our children from adversity by removing the frustrating experience or solving the problem for them, that places them on a path of learned helplessness where they would be unable, or unwilling, to stick at problems and solve things on their own. When you observe your child grappling with a task they find challenging, you could say something like, "I can see learning to tie your shoelaces is really tricky for you. Keep going, I know your patience and practice will help you build those connections in your brain and it will become easy."

5. EMBRACE AND CELEBRATE FAILURE

Instead of being ashamed of their failures, encourage your children to embrace, and even celebrate failing. You can frame it in a fun way explaining that FAIL simply means First Attempt In Learning and that when they fail at something they are essentially moving forward because they can learn from their mistakes. Ask questions like, "What did you learn from this?" or "What would you do differently next time?" I like the idea of Failure Fridays (the Big Life Journal has more ideas about this) where everyone in the family celebrates how they've learned through their mistakes throughout the week. This way, your children come to realise that we all make mistakes and see them as a normal part of learning and growing.

Areas for reflection

1. How was failure viewed in your family when you were growing up? Has this impacted on your view of failure as an adult? Has it impacted on how you help your children deal with failure?

2. Do you see failure as a positive opportunity to grow, or as a negative experience that is an obstacle to success that is to be avoided? Consider the message this is sending to your children about their failures and setbacks.

3. Consider the last time you tried something new, and it was difficult or frustrating, or even when you tried something and failed. What thoughts went through your head? Did you feel incompetent? Did your anxiety levels rise, and you just wanted to give up? If you answered yes to those questions, these thoughts are an indicator of a fixed mindset. That is okay as long as you recognise it.

IN A NUTSHELL

★ Failure provides children with benefits they cannot receive in any other way. It teaches them how to adapt and change the way they do things, learn about what didn't work and persist with tasks that are difficult and sometimes frustrating.

★ Protecting children from failure has been recognised to increase their vulnerability to emotional distress and future experiences of failure.

★ To develop resilience in our kids, we need to help them learn from their mistakes and failures and reframe them as an opportunity to learn, grow and improve.

CHAPTER NINE
Working on self-mastery

For children, mastery entails struggle. This means they must be permitted to struggle.

Nathaniel Branden

"No! I do it! My turn!" We have all heard toddlers asserting their independence with unyielding resolve. They will try by any method necessary to establish and claim their autonomy. They are driven to independently succeed in achieving their goal and won't let any adult stand in their way. This often seems to happen in the middle of a crowded store in front of large groups of people. As embarrassing, uncomfortable and awkward as these situations can be, they are the beginning of children developing self-mastery.

Children crave chances to demonstrate their competence. They love to help and do things adults do. Whenever I was carrying a box or moving something around the house, Mitchell (who was six at the time), wanted to help me even if it meant just placing his hand on the side of the box I was carrying. He wasn't bearing any of the weight, but through his eyes, he was doing the same thing as I was and was helping me – for a child that's a very big deal. Another example of competence is from one of my five-year-old students at school. He had learnt how to click his fingers to the Addams Family song we used to learn the days of the week. He was incredibly proud of this achievement and wanted to 'teach' the other kids in my class how to do it too, as he had seen me doing it when we sang the song as a class.

Dr Jim Taylor, in his book *Your Children are Listening*, defines self-mastery as the ability to motivate yourself to consistently behave in ways that move you towards your goals rather than away from them, to set a course of action and keep moving forward no matter how hard it becomes. He explains that in order to successfully reach their goals, children need to master skills and believe they can competently manage their environment and achieve what they want to accomplish.

Childhood is when the essential belief 'I am a competent person' is embedded.

Whether it be as they first reach out and grasp your finger when they are tiny, learning to walk, talk, feed themselves or dress themselves, all of these activities lay the foundations for their future beliefs about their ability to master the world in which they live.

As a teacher, I've frequently observed my students trying to do things themselves, not asking for their parents' help. All of a sudden, their parents try to help whether it's to make things easier for their child, out of expediency or because they realise that their children can't quite accomplish the task they're trying to do alone. My heart fills with pride when I see those parents rebuffed with an "I can do it myself" and a renewed sense of determination. It's a potent lesson that your child is willing to work hard and work at developing their skills, and intervening too early often sends the message that you don't think they can do it.

As a guidance counsellor in schools, I often observed children who had internalised a sense of incompetence. I've seen them in classrooms, on playgrounds and on sports teams. They often have a pessimistic outlook on life saying things like, "I can't do it" or "I'm not gonna be able to do that." They can be fearful and reluctant to even try, saying things like, "No, I'm afraid and don't want to do that." Undoubtedly some of these children were born with cautious or apprehensive temperaments. For others, I can see why they haven't developed a sense of competence by observing their parents who are anxious, worried, overly protective and intrusive. They intervene at the first suggestion of difficulties, apparently concerned that these challenges and possible failures will damage their child's confidence and self-esteem.

These parents frequently perceive danger everywhere and communicate that idea to their children. They prohibit their children from taking even benign risks and linger over them, swooping in at the first sign of distress, frustration or potential injury. They are, of course, well-intentioned and believe they are doing what is best for their child. What they are doing is unconsciously conveying the message that the world is a dangerous place, and that they don't believe their children are capable of handling that, which undermines their children's confidence, sense of competence and willingness to take appropriate risks.

> As both a parent and teacher, I have found the greatest obstacle to providing these naturally occurring opportunities to develop competence is our lack of time.

It's frequently just quicker, easier, a lot less frustrating and sometimes less messy, to do it ourselves. From our perspective, allowing our children to help wash the dog, make dinner, bake a cake or do the washing up is often more trouble than it's worth. I know I often found it easier to simply do things for Mitchell when he was learning, especially if we had to be somewhere in a hurry, rather than patiently waiting until he had completed the task independently. It took up more time, was harder than if I simply did it and frequently it didn't turn out as well as if I'd just done it. But I knew that for Mitchell, these experiences, and the sense of competence and mastery that emerged from them, would provide him with a strong foundation of self-efficacy. Children begin to believe in their ability to succeed and accomplish tasks; they view themselves as competent, capable and powerful and are more likely to exhibit resilience in the face of setbacks.

Encouraging autonomy and mastery requires lots of patience, so as parents, we need to remain flexible and plan ahead. I remember when Mitchell decided he wanted to tie his own shoelaces independently. Initially, it took what seemed to be forever; he wouldn't accept any help at all and needed the opportunity to try time and time again. But within a short amount of time, he gained mastery of the task and moved on to different things. When activities take time, or are challenging for children to accomplish, we often take over and do it for them. But it's in that struggle that growth takes place, and every time they develop mastery, it builds their confidence and resilience.

By providing our children with opportunities to experience mastery, competence and autonomy, we are fostering their independence, critical thinking, problem-solving and independence.

1.   PROVIDE OPPORTUNITIES TO PRACTISE

As parents, we need to provide our children with a wide variety of opportunities so they can feel capable and competent. Opportunities such as putting their toys away, making their bed, brushing their teeth, tidying their room, carrying their dishes to the kitchen. These opportunities don't always have to be time-pressured – you could draw an outline of a pair of shoes on a piece of cardboard, punch holes in for where the laces go, thread laces through those holes and then let your child practice tying those up. You could give them a child-sized broom, dustpan and brush so they can help clean up any mess they find around the house or give them a child-sized watering can so they can help you water plants around the house and in the garden. Kids develop an optimistic, can-do attitude when they feel capable and are trusted to get the job done.

2.   TEACH GOAL SETTING

Teaching our kids how to set reasonable goals and develop strategies for achieving those goals supports them in experiencing greater self-mastery. One of the simplest ways to explain goals to children is by linking it to a concept they are already familiar with such as playing sports. You can describe a goal as being a target, something you aim at or shoot for just like in basketball, soccer or hockey. Explain how planning what you want to achieve at school, at home or in sport is called goal setting and helps people succeed in achieving what they want. Teach them that goals usually start with 'I will' and have two parts. The first is about what they want to accomplish and the second part is when they want to accomplish it by. Then encourage them to identify different ways they can achieve their goals and consider various solutions for the challenges they experience on the way to success. This helps them experience greater hope and optimism that they will be successful at achieving the goal. Finally, discuss the purpose of their goal with them asking questions like why would you like to achieve that? What would the benefit be?

I helped Mitchell understand how to set goals when he was learning to ride his bike. His goal – I want to learn to ride my bike by summer holidays so I can go riding with my friends. We talked about how he could practise riding, what challenges might come up, for example, falling off and hurting himself and how he would overcome these. He achieved the goal and spent his summer holidays happily riding around the neighbourhood basking in his success. Children may set very easy goals to achieve. This is okay, as if they can accomplish them by themselves, they will gain a sense of mastery and competence that will encourage them to set a more challenging goal next time because they experienced that success.

3. PROVIDE SCAFFOLDING

When we think about scaffolding, it's often in reference to the construction of buildings. We see the scaffolding go up to support the building while it's being built, and then the scaffolding is taken away once it's finished. This is the same thing we can do for our kids when we provide them with just enough support when they are learning, practising and applying new skills and information, so they tackle different challenges confidently. It allows them to move from their current level of understanding and skill to a more advanced one. An example of scaffolding is beginning with the training wheels for a bike, then our steadying hand when the training wheels come off before we then release the bike and our children ride on their own.

4. KEEP AN ADVENTURE JOURNAL

Encourage your child to try new things, do things in a different way, change strategies if something isn't working and take small risks with you there as a support and safety net just in case they need some extra help. They need to develop the skills to make sensible decisions and manage risks for themselves. A great movie to watch that encourages adventures and risk-taking is the movie *Up*. Of course, the risks need to be age-appropriate for your child, such as climbing a tree or the supervised use of tools such as hammers and nails. It is much better for them to learn how to manage risks and adventures when they're younger than when they are 16 and thinking of getting into a car with a friend who has been drinking. Either you or your kids can write about the new adventures they've had in the journal.

5. RISKY ACTIVITIES

Let kids take part in age-appropriate, well-supervised risky activities such as hammering nails into a piece of wood, cutting up bananas, watermelon or apples with butter knives, climbing trees in the back yard or at playgrounds rather than just using the play equipment, helping build a fire and then toasting marshmallows. All of these activities help kids develop confidence, strengthen their decision-making skills and provide them with opportunities to develop mastery.

Areas for reflection

1. Did you have opportunities throughout your childhood to develop autonomy and mastery? How are you providing these for your children?

2. Can you remember a time in your childhood when you took a risk? What was great about it? What did you learn?

3. The next time you feel frustrated or angry when your kids are taking a long time to try something new, ask yourself, "Why am I feeling this?" Remember your thoughts are your interpretation about what is happening and what should be happening. Try taking a deep breath or stepping back and recognising the learning that's happening for your child. (I recognise that's sometimes easier said than done).

IN A NUTSHELL

★   As parents, it is our responsibility to provide many opportunities for our children to develop autonomy, competence and self-mastery as these attributes strengthen their resilience, sense of self-worth and self-efficacy.

★   When children believe that they can succeed in mastering a skill and learning new things, even if it is as simple as dressing themselves, doing up buttons or getting their own breakfast, they are more likely to develop grit by persevering towards reaching their goal, learning from their mistakes and not giving up when something doesn't work out the way they'd hoped.

★   When we allow our children to take risks, experience failure and feel frustrated, we provide them with opportunities to develop skills of resilience and cope within a safe, loving and supportive environment.

CHAPTER TEN
Practising mindfulness

Between stimulus and response, there is a space. In that space lies our freedom and power to choose our response. In our response lies our growth and freedom.

Victor Frankl

We're trying to raise resilient kids but struggle with the immense pressures of life in our extraordinarily fast-paced pressure-cooker society where we are all hyperconnected and yet often still lonely. Life is a lot more uncertain than when we were growing up and presents a myriad of physical, emotional and mental health challenges for both parents and kids. Many of us are just surviving and are unsure about the best ways to develop our children's mental fitness muscles so that they can grow into resilient, happy tweens and teens.

I'm not sure if you've ever experienced this, but I have had days when I've hopped into my car and driven from one place to another, quite some distance at times, and not been able to remember how I arrived at my destination. I had been driving on automatic pilot without being in the present moment and aware of what I was doing – I simply drove the car out of habit. We can also go through life this way, often being miles away in our thoughts and not truly 'present' in the moment without being aware that this is happening.

Human beings tend to be reactive; our amygdala, one of the primitive parts of the brain's limbic system, keeps us safe by responding to threats whenever it thinks we are in danger. This can be actual physical danger or psychological and emotional danger. For example, when we are afraid that people aren't going to like us or when someone says something that is hurtful, we can react in either a fight, flight or freeze mode. Sometimes in these situations, we may say or do something that we wish we could take back the moment after we blurt it out or do it.

> Mindfulness supports us to create space between our emotions and our actions.

We can learn how to pay attention to our feelings and thoughts so that we can deal with positive and negative experiences more calmly and make better decisions. It helps us observe what is happening in our bodies in the present moment, understand what is driving our behaviour and choose actions that are based on clear thinking.

As a guidance counsellor, I worked with many educators who were embedding mindfulness practices in their classrooms to help their students improve their focus, deal with their emotions and regulate their behaviour. These educators recognised the growing number of students impacted by stress and anxiety and wanted to give the children in their classrooms tools and strategies to cope with life.

They started by explaining what mindfulness was to their students and then established different mindfulness practices throughout the day. These educators reported that they had observed changes in the children in their classes who would normally present as quite anxious or stressed. When the students applied their mindfulness tools and strategies the educators saw a decrease in behaviours that displayed stress and anxiety. The children were more focused and calm, could self-regulate better and were more empathic towards their peers.

One of the kindergarten teachers I was working with at school had started to teach her students about how they could calm their minds by using mindfulness jars. She explained that their minds were sometimes full of thoughts swirling around like the glitter in the jar, especially if they were upset or cross about something. Then she taught them some mindfulness techniques and explained that using these techniques helped their minds to calm down and stop swirling, just like when she set the jar down all the glitter settled to the bottom and the water became clear. One day when I was visiting the classroom after first break, the teacher came into the classroom looking frazzled and was short with the class as she asked them to sit on the carpet. One of the little girls in the class ran and got her mindfulness jar, then took it to the teacher saying, "Miss, it looks like there are lots of things swirling in your head. You need to watch my mindfulness jar so they can settle down." These kindergarten students knew what it felt and looked like when their heads were swirling with thoughts and feelings as well as recognising when other people's minds were swirling.

The purpose of teaching our children mindfulness practices is to provide them with skills and tools that support them in recognising that their thoughts are 'just thoughts' and that these thoughts can pass. We wanted to help them develop an awareness of both their inner and outer experiences by identifying and understanding how emotions can manifest and feel in their bodies and to recognise when their attention has wandered.

We can help them focus their attention and awareness on the present moment, and provide scaffolding and support so they can recognise, acknowledge and accept their feelings, thoughts and sensations in their body without judging them as right or wrong.

When I am working with children, I explain that mindfulness is about noticing what is happening right now in this present moment. It's about taking notice of how their body feels and what they can see, hear, smell, touch and taste. I talk about how they can feel different emotions in their body – maybe it gets tight somewhere when they are angry, or they feel like they have butterflies in their tummy when they're anxious or nervous, or it could even be a good sensation. I encourage them to notice what their mind is doing and thinking, and how this impacts on their feelings and their body. When they pay mindful attention to what is happening around them and inside their bodies, it can help children calm down when they are angry, sad or frustrated and help them deal with big tough emotions. When working with children and young people who are stressed and have developed a high level of anxiety, I help them realise that while a little bit of worrying and stress is normal, there are helpful mindfulness tools and strategies they can use to decrease their stress and anxiety.

Karen Hooker, Jeremy Wardle, Maureen Weinhardt and Hunter Clarke-Fields have all found that mindfulness practices can:

* help reduce children's symptoms of stress, anxiety and depression
* mitigate the effects of bullying
* help improve their capacity to regulate their emotions

✶   help them sleep better

✶   improve academic performance

✶   boost their confidence, optimism and positive emotions

✶   develop increased compassion and kindness

✶   develop stronger relationships and improved mental
    fitness and wellbeing.

As parents, we are uniquely positioned to help our children develop mindfulness habits early in life that will inform their behaviours as an adult.

> These mindfulness tools and strategies can help them create a space between their emotions and their actions so they can choose to proactively respond to life's challenges rather than reactively responding to difficult situations and big emotions.

However, mindfulness is not a cure-all for our children's behaviours that push our buttons such as whining, fighting with their siblings, tantrums or arguing back. Even if both we and our children practise mindfulness, we can still experience difficult, challenging emotions and negative mental chatter that clouds our thinking and cause us to reactively respond to events. When we implement our mindfulness tools and strategies, we can change our relationships with our thoughts, emotions and negative self-talk so they won't have the same impact on us and our behaviour.

There are many fun and easy ways we can begin introducing mindfulness to our kids. If you want to introduce mindfulness to your kids for the first time, choose a time when they are calm. If they want to run around and play because they're full of energy, it's better to let them do that and choose a different time. It's also important for us as parents and teachers to choose age-appropriate mindfulness practices and tools, and I have provided a variety of ideas that you can choose from to suit your individual needs and family context.

1. LISTENING TO A SOUND

This is one of the first ways I introduce a mindfulness activity to young children. I hold a small Tibetan singing bowl (you could use a bell or a phone app that has different sounds on it) and explain that I am going to tap the bowl and it will make a sound and then ask them to listen carefully until they can't hear the sound anymore (this is usually 30 seconds to a minute). I've found that this exercise has a calming effect on the students and they think it's quite fun. It focuses their attention, and we can then move on to other mindfulness activities.

2. FOCUSED BELLY BREATHING

Ask your kids to lie down flat on their backs and gently put either a book, a stuffed animal or a small stone on their belly. Then ask them to focus their attention on their breathing, watching the book, animal or stone rise and fall as they breathe in and out. I also use triangle breathing to help older kids focus on their breath. I ask them to make a triangle with their forefingers and thumbs and then breathe into their belly for three counts (that represents one side of the triangle), then hold their breath for three counts (that's another side of the triangle) and then breathe out for three counts as the last side of the triangle. This encourages them to focus on slowing their breathing down.

Other ways to encourage belly breathing are by blowing bubbles or pinwheels. Remind the kids to focus on taking deep, slow breaths and then exhaling slowly, so they can fill the bubbles or make the pinwheel turn for as long as possible (watch that they don't become lightheaded doing this). Ask them to closely watch the bubbles as they form and either float away or burst.

3. CREATE A MINDFULNESS JAR

Choose a clear glass jar, like a Mason jar, and fill it almost all the way with water. Then add a large spoonful of dry glitter to the water. Put the lid on the jar and shake it around, making the glitter swirl. Once you've done that you can show it to your kids, if they haven't been helping you make it, and talk to them about how the glitter represents their thoughts and mind when they are feeling angry, frustrated, stressed or anxious.

When the glitter is swirling around, it's hard to see clearly. This is similar to when their thoughts are swirling; it's hard to think clearly and easy to make foolish decisions because they're upset. Explain that this is normal and happens to adults too.

Then put the jar down in front of them and ask them to watch what happens when the jar is still. The glitter starts to settle to the bottom, and it's easier to see things because the water is becoming clearer. Talk to them about how our minds work the same way and that when we can be still and calm for a while, our brains start to calm down, our thoughts settle down, and we can see things in a clearer way.

I have used this with many students ranging in ages from four to 12, and all of them love the idea, as well as the activity of making their jars. These students understood the concept and had tools and strategies they could use to help calm their brains.

4. BODY SCAN

One of the core practices of mindfulness is a body scan that alerts children to what they are feeling in their bodies, as well as how they can relax all the muscles in their bodies. Ask your kids to lie down on their backs and close their eyes. Then direct them to squeeze every muscle in their body as tight as they can. Tell them to squeeze their toes and feet, squeeze their hands into fists, and make their legs and arms as hard as stone. Then, after a few seconds, have them release all their muscles and relax for a few minutes. You can also talk them through tightening and relaxing different parts of their body. For older children you can ask them to scan their bodies and identify where they are holding different feelings, stress or tension – they might be able to tell you this by describing the sensations they feel in those areas.

5. BEDTIME RITUALS

You can develop all types of mindfulness rituals that soothe your children before bed. One I used with Mitchell was to do a short body scan meditation after we had read a bedtime story and before he went to sleep. I'd ask him to close his eyes and bring his attention to his toes, feet, legs, tummy and other parts of his body and think about those areas. This helped to calm both his body and his mind. There are lots of guided meditation Apps you can choose from, and some of these are listed in the Resources section at the back of the book.

Areas for reflection

1. Do you often wake up and rush to move forward with your day, switching on your devices as soon as you can? If this sounds like you, experiment with starting your day in a more present and mindful way and see how it feels.

2. People often think that multitasking will get more done. Are you often trying to do lots of things at the same time and cram as much in as possible? Does it feel like your brain is about to burst at the seams and is overflowing with information, thoughts and feelings? Draw a picture of what it's like to feel this way and then draw a picture of what it's like to feel focused and calm. Which do you prefer – Mind Full or Mindful?

3. How mindful are you when you're eating? My husband sometimes calls me the hoover because I eat so quickly. Do you eat mindfully and really savour your food? Give it a go and see what you notice.

IN A NUTSHELL

★   Mindfulness is the skill of focusing your attention on the present moment, noticing what's around you, what you're doing, who you're talking to, how you're feeling. When we pay attention to what is happening, it helps us and our children to more accurately assess and respond to situations and people.

★   When we practise mindfulness, we induce the relaxation response, which is the physiological opposite to the stress response. Mindfulness calms and quietens our body and nervous system, which helps us think more clearly and function more effectively.

★   Everyone's mind naturally wanders; in fact, our mind wanders almost 50 per cent of the time, so please don't stress if your children find mindfulness activities challenging at first. The good news is it's just like going to the gym – the more you, and they, practise the better they will become at keeping their attention and focus in the present moment.

CONCLUSION
Making memories together

The key question to keep asking is: Are you spending your time on the right things? As time is all you have.

Randy Pausch

One of my most valued things in the entire world is a tin lunch box filled with keepsakes, cards and photos. I open it up whenever I need a boost or am feeling a little down, and these things always bring a smile to my face and possibly a small tear to my eye. If ever there was a fire at my house that would be one of the first things I'd grab. Good memories are our psychological equivalent to those magical boxes we turn to when we need an emotional boost. Those magic moments that touch our hearts and delight our souls may seem trivial to others, but the memory of them consistently provides a boost of positive emotion that lifts us out of sadness and desolation.

> Memories from childhood are some of the most precious we have as they shape our lives and have a significant impact on the kind of people we become.

Research has shown that people who have childhoods filled with experiences imbued with joy, love and fun have a more optimistic disposition as well as better health later in life. It's our job as parents to help our children make quality memories they will treasure forever.

These memories don't necessarily have to be of expensive gifts; very few of my childhood memories revolve around gifts that I received. I definitely remember the year that I received a cabbage patch doll, as well as my brother and I opening books from our grandparents every year. But other than that, my gift-receiving recollections are quite scant. It's not that I didn't appreciate the gifts I was given, I did, it's just that the most treasured memories I have are of spending time with family and the experiences we had together.

Magic moments don't have to be militarily precision-planned – they can be tiny, impromptu fun-filled moments where there is no agenda, no great rush. They're just enjoyment, fun, laughter at something only the two of you find funny, a glorious sunrise together or time just before bed.

Good memories are a magical button our children can press to play back all those good times and reset their minds into a positive state. We can be the magicians in our children's lives creating magic moments they will look back on, times when they felt enveloped in a blanket of love, when they felt understood and had a deep-seated sense of belonging and connection.

Many of these magic moments are the result of accident or pure luck and circumstance, but there are things we can do, with a little effort and awareness on our part, to create memories that will last a lifetime for our kids. They may require our time and energy, but they don't have to be taxing or emotionally draining. I am the first one to acknowledge that there were days when all I could do was make sure Mitchell was clean, fed and out the door to school as I dashed to work, and creating memories was the last thing on my mind. I had to make a concerted effort to develop habits and routines of connection that helped me create those memories that he still talks about now.

Our kids' lives are frequently very structured and scheduled these days with school, after-school activities, extra classes and sports on the weekends.

> Sometimes we just need to hop off the treadmill, forget the daily routine and let both ourselves and our kids relax away from the unending grind.

Decide to do something fun as a family and let the kids plan what to do for a day. Take unexpected trips to different places; it doesn't have to be expensive. Find some interesting places around your hometown, this changes things up and is something they will remember and talk about fondly in years to come. We used to have a day in our house that was called 'Super Happy Fun Day' where we put aside everything else and spent the day doing whatever made us happy, whatever we enjoyed and whatever made us laugh. These days were some of the happiest memories we created together.

One of the key things we need to do is to view every interaction as an opportunity to connect and make magic memories. Slowing down and sharing moments with our kids: stopping to listen to their laughter, or their breathing as you peek in on them before you go to bed, going to sporting events, plays or concerts, really looking at nature with them as they ask you to consider the ants' nest or ladybird they just found. Being with them in the present moment and helping them savour it so they can remember those moments for the rest of their lives.

Any adult in the life of a child has a profound capacity to make a positive impact, just like you can, right now.

No matter what role you play in the village that surrounds our little people, you, definitely you, can make a difference. You can choose in this moment to start, one small strategy at a time, building kids who bounce, who are grounded in a strong sense of self, who have rituals and strategies that build their mental fitness.

To give them the strength they need to navigate an ever-changing world. To stop our children believing, when they should just be children, that there is no point to living. And ultimately, to stop the parental heartbreak I am witness to every single day when our little people crumble.

My hope is that this book has resonated with you, provided some guidance for you and equipped you to strengthen your children's mental fitness muscles. We are fortunate to have this opportunity to teach our kids the skills and strategies they need to become confident, kind, loving, mentally fit human beings. When our kids live these positive habits of mind every day, they will become second nature to them just like putting on sunscreen is now. Their brains will become hardwired to effectively navigate their way around, or through, various crises life may throw their way. This is how we go about raising a mentally fit generation.

Extra resources for help

Picture books are an ideal way to introduce concepts to children and start developing their mental fitness muscles. Books play a critical role in children's lives. They can help children learn how to empathise with others by empathising with the characters they read about. Kids can observe characters in books going through hard times and overcoming them and possibly see themselves reflected in those stories. Books can provide a vocabulary for kids struggling to articulate how they feel, and can let them know that other people feel that way too sometimes. Reading together builds connection and closeness between parent and child, provides a shared vocabulary for family life and makes memories that children will cherish for a lifetime. Reading does not have to be an expensive activity – many families I work with plan weekly trips to the library where they have fun selecting books together.

The following books provide a good starting point to explore the concepts covered in each of the chapters.

Chapter one: Teaching brain basics

Your Fantastic Elastic Brain: Stretch It, Shape It by JoAnn Deak

A Walk in the Rain with a Brain by Edward M Hallowell

Bubble Gum Brain by Julia Cook

Chapter two: Cultivating optimism

Grumpy Pants by Claire Messer

The Bad Mood by Moritz Petz

Move Your Mood by Brenda Miles

The Happiest Book Ever by Bob Shea

Pete the Cat and His Magic Sunglasses by James Dean

Think Happy by Nancy Carlson

Chapter three: Managing emotions

Understanding feelings

The Way I Feel by Janan Cain

The Grouchy Ladybug by Eric Carle

Alexander and the Terrible, Horrible, No Good, Very Bad Day by Judith Viorst

The Unbudgeable Curmudgeon by Matt Burgess

The Feelings Book by Todd Parr

When Sadness is at Your Door by Eva Eland

All Kinds of Feelings by Sheri Safran

My Many Coloured Days by Dr Seuss

In My Heart: A book of feelings by Jo Witek

The Colour Monster by Anna Llenas

There Are No Animals in This Book (Only Feelings) by Chani Sanchez

Theo's Mood by Maryanne Cocca-Leffler

A Book of Feelings by Amanda McCardie

The Great Big Book of Feelings by Mary Hoffman

The Quiet Book by Deborah Underwood

Today I Feel Silly and Other Moods That Make My Day by Jamie Lee Curtis

Feelings by Aliki

Grumpy Monkey by Suzanne Lang

What to Do When You're Feeling Blue by Andi Cann

Visiting Feelings by Lauren Rubenstein

Yarralin by Janne Hardy and Sue Langley

Feeling scared

The Fun Book of Scary Stuff by Emily Jenkins

The Dark by Lemony Snickett

Scaredy Squirrel by Emily Watt

Nana in the City by Lauren Castillo

Thundercake by Patricia Polacco

Courage by Bernard Waber

Max the Brave by Ed Vere

When I'm Feeling Scared by Trace Moroney

Little Mouse's Big Book of Fears by Emily Gravatt

The I'm Not Scared Book by Todd Parr

Brave As Can Be: A Book of Courage by Jo Witek

Managing anger and other big feelings

When Sophie Gets Angry – Really, Really Angry
by Molly Bang

When I'm Feeling Angry by Trace Moroney

When I feel Angry by Cornelia Maude Spelman

When Miles Got Mad by Sam Kurtzman-Counter

Mad Isn't Bad by Mundy Micahelene

How to Take the GRRR Out of Anger by Elizabeth Verdick

Don't Rant and Rave on Wednesday by Adolph Moser

What to Do When Your Temper Flares by Dawn Huebner

The Snurtch by Sean Ferrell

Sally Simon Simmons' Super Frustrating Day
by Abbie Schiller

Zach Gets Frustrated by William Mulcahy

Crankenstein by Samantha Berger

Jack's Worry by Sam Zupardi

Wemberley Worried by Kevin Henkes

Beautiful Oops by Barney Saltzberg

You are Strong by Danielle Dufayet

Crabbypants by Julie Gassman

Harriet, You'll Drive Me Wild by Mem Fox

Developing problem-solving skills

What Do You Do With a Problem? By Kobi Yamada

Dough Knights and Dragons by Dee Leone

Rosie Revere, Engineer by Andrea Beatty

Duncan the Story Dragon by Amada Driscoll

The Templeton Twins Have an Idea by Ellis Weiner

The Whale in My Swimming Pool by Joyce Wan

Russell the Sheep by Rob Scotten

A Little Stuck by Oliver Jeffers

Chapter four: Recognising strengths

Tomorrow I'll Be Brave by Jessica Hische

All the Ways to Be Smart by Davina Bell

Giraffes Can't Dance by Giles Andreae

The Book of Gold by Bob Staake

We're All Wonders by R.J. Palacio

Call it Courage by Armstrong Sperry

What's Right with This Picture? Teaching kids about character strengths through stories by Renee Jain

True You: Authentic Strengths for Kids by Fatima Doman

The Little Book of Character Strengths by June Rousso

See the Good: Reinforce Your Child's Character Strengths by Niina Melanen

Chapter five: Making friends

How to be a friend

How to Be a Friend: A Guide to Making Friends and Keeping Them by Laurie Krasny Brown and Marc Brown

Should I Share My Ice-cream? By Mo Willems

Pearl Barley and Charlie Parsley by Aaron Blabey

The Conversation Train by Joel Shaul

Leonardo the Terrible Monster by Mo Willems

Quackers by Liz Wong

I Just Ate My Friend by Heidi McKinnon

The Rainbow Fish by Marcus Pfister

Bear's New Friend by Karma Wilson

The Berenstain Bears and the Trouble With Friends by Stan Berenstain

Making Friends Is an Art by Julia Cook

Do You Want to Be My Friend? by Eric Carle

How to cope with bullies

Bad Apple: A Tale of Friendship by Edward Hemingway

The Juicebox Bully by Bob Sornson and Maria Dismondy

Stick and Stone by Beth Ferry

Stand Tall Molly Lou Melon by Patty Lovell

The Recess Queen by Alexis O'Neill and Laura Huliska Beith

I Walk With Vanessa by Kerascoët

Enemy Pie by Derek Munson

Llama Llama and the Bully Goat by Anna Dewdney

Bully by Patricia Polaco

The Bully Blockers Club by Teresa Bateman

Marlene, Marlene, Queen of the Mean by Jane Lynch

When friends are upset

My Friend is Sad by Mo Willems

Boy + Bot by Amy Dyckman

Wilfred Gordon McDonald Partridge by Mem Fox

A Ball for Daisy by Chris Raschka

Square Cat by Elizabeth Schoonmaker

A Sick Day for Amos McGee by Philip C. Stead

That's What Friends Are For by Valeri Gorbachev

When children find it difficult to make friends

Bird, Balloon, Bear by Il Sung Na

The Adventures of Beekle: The Unimaginary Friend by Dan Santant

Shy by Deborah Freedman

Strictly No Elephants by Lisa Mantchev

No One Likes a Fart by Zoe Foster Blake

Big Friends by Linda Sarah

The New Kid by Marie Louise Fitzpatrick

Chapter six: Encouraging kindness and empathy

The Invisible Boy by Trudy Ludwig

Last Stop on Market Street by Matt De La Pena

Those Shoes by Maribeth Boelts

You, Me and Empathy by Jayneen Sanders

Come With Me by Holly M. Mcghee

Be Kind by Pat Zietlow Miller

Have You Filled a Bucket Today? by Carol Mccloud

The Monster Who Lost His Mean by Tiffany Strelitz

Hey, Little Ant by Phillip and Hannah Hoose

Empathy is My Superpower by Bryan Smith

Kindness is Cooler Mrs Ruler by Margery Cuyler

Horton Hears a Who by Dr Seuss

Strictly No Elephants by Lisa Mantchev

Nerdy Birdy by Aaron Reynolds

I Walk with Vanessa by Kerascoët

The Big Umbrella by Amy June Bates

A Sick Day for Amos McGee by Phillip C Stead

What Does it Mean to Be Kind? by Rana DiOrio

Good People Everywhere by Lynea Gillen

Should I Share My Ice-cream? by Mo Willems

Plant a Kiss by Amy Krouse Rosenthal

We Don't Eat Our Classmates by Ryan T. Higgins

Chapter seven: Fostering gratitude

Thankful by Eileen Spinelli

Bear Says Thanks by Karma Wilson

Thanks a Million by Nikki Grimes

Those Shoes by Maribeth Boelts

An Awesome Book of Thanks by Dallas Clayton

The Berenstain Bears Count their Blessings by Stan and Jan Berenstain

Gracious Thanks by Pat Mora

The Thankful Book by Todd Parr

Gratitude Soup by Olivia Rosewood

Apple Cake: A Gratitude by Dawn Casey

Thank You Mr Panda by Steve Antony

Did I Ever Tell You How Lucky You Are? by Dr Seuss

The Scribblybark Tree and the Dragon by Janne Hardy and Sue Langley

Chapter eight: Learning to fail

Making a Splash – Growth Mindset for Kids by Carol E. Reiley

My Day is Ruined! A Story Teaching Flexible Thinking by Bryan Smith

Good News, Bad News by Jeff Mack

Thanks For the Feedback, I Think by Julia Cook

Sometimes You Win, Sometimes You Learn For Kids by John C Maxwell

When Pigs Fly by Valerie Coulman

I Made a Aistake by Miriam Nerlove

Nobody is Perfick by Bernard Waber

The Thing Lou Couldn't Do by Ashley Spires

Mistakes That Worked by Charlotte Foltz Jones

Chapter nine: Working on self-mastery

The Little Engine That Could by Watty Piper

Everyone Can Learn to Ride a Bicycle by Chris Raschka

My Brave Year of Firsts by Jamie Lee Curtis

Shark Nate-O by Tara Lubebe and Becky Cattie

Matilda by Roald Dahl

Chapter ten: Practising mindfulness

Puppy Mind by Andrew Jordan Nance

What Does It Mean to Be Present? by Rana DiOrio

Sitting Still Like a Frog by Eline Snel

Moody Cow Meditates by Kerry Lee MacLean

Peaceful Piggy Meditation by Kerry Lee MacLean

The Mindful Dragon by Steve Herman

Mind Bubbles by Heather Krantz

Listening to My Body by Gabi Garcia

Listening With My Heart by Gabi Garcia

A Handful of Quiet: Happiness in Four Pebbles by Tich Nhat Hanh

The Lemonade Hurricane: A Story of Mindfulness and Meditation by Licia Morelli

Breathe Like a Bear: 30 Mindful Moments for Kids to Feel Calm and Focused Anytime, Anywhere by Kira Willey

ABC Mindful Me by Christiane Engel

My Brain is a Thinking Machine by Candice T. Aguirre

Meditations for kids

There are a wide variety of different apps and websites that provide guided meditations you can do with children of all ages. These are some of the best ones I have found.

Kidevolve www.kidevolve.com

Headspace for kids www.headspace.com/meditation/kids

Insight Timer www.insighttimer.com

Smiling Mind www.smilingmind.com.au

Breathe, Think, Do Sesame – app

Calm – app

Breathing Bubbles – app

Dreamy Kid – app

About the author

Kari is a national and international author, speaker and a mental fitness expert with a special interest in the early childhood years. She is on a mission to change the conversation about how we promote and protect our children's mental health and wellbeing.

Kari started her career as a teacher. Graduating in the early 90s she began her career working with children who had suffered significant abuse, undertaking research with colleagues about the effects this had on their social and emotional wellbeing and how this could be ameliorated. This research, combined with her work with thousands of children, parents and educators, and 22 years of volunteering with Camp Quality, cultivated her passion to support families and educators to build mental fitness and resilience in kids.

After studying in 2003 with the founder of Positive Psychology, Dr Martin Seligman, Kari began implementing this new science into her work as a teacher and guidance counsellor. Having embedded the learning into her life and work, she brings an in-depth understanding of how to foster children's mental fitness. Kari translates complex research into practical, easy to use tools and strategies that plant the seeds of resilience, emotional wellbeing and mental fitness in our children.

She has spoken at over 150 events both in Australia and internationally, worked with over 300 schools and delivered over 500 workshops for businesses, educators, early childhood professionals, carers and mental health practitioners.

Kari's books and resources have been called insightful, impactful and essential in saving our next and most important generation. She leaves her audience with practical, actionable tips they can immediately use to help their kids thrive.

To connect with Kari you can find her at:

* www.karisutton.com
* Facebook: Kari Sutton – Author, Speaker, Educator
* Instagram: @karisuttoninsta

Acknowledgements

Writing a book is way more demanding than it may appear. It requires endless hours of deep research, crafting, shaping, editing as well as significant support both personally and professionally. The process of writing a book is not a one-person game and I would like to take this opportunity to thank the team who helped me move this project across the finish line.

The first thank you must go to Megan Dalla-Camina, my first book coach, who was able to see potential in an idea that I had been turning over in my head and helped me formulate those ideas into a defined project. The next major thank-you is to Kelly Irving, my book advisor and first editor – her decades of experience helped me shape a big bunch of research and practical hands-on experience into a book. Her incredibly generous support and skilful pruning of my words was crucial, and I am forever grateful. To my amazing final editor Karen Comer who helped me turn my manuscript that had potential into the polished book you now have in your hands. Thank you both for not settling for good when excellent was within our reach and I know it is going to help so many families.

There is an extensive list of people who have made this book a reality and contributed in many diverse ways. I would like to thank Jacqueline Nagle, my business mentor, who saw the value in my work and message when she met me in 2015 and convinced me to start crafting it in my own unique way. To Paula Robinson, thank you for sharing your wisdom and urging me to explore how we can proactively embed the intentional habits of mental fitness into our children's lives. I would also like to thank Sue Langley for encouraging me to write this book and sharing her enthusiasm for the book's ability to fill a gap in the literature.

I am also extremely grateful to the families who have so freely shared their stories and struggles with me, letting me into their world and giving me permission to share their stories with you.

Thank you to the schools, teachers and early childhood educators who have shared their stories with me and have enthusiastically embraced the book already. I look forward to delivering many more parent nights in the coming months and years.

While writing this book I have come to even more deeply appreciate the vital role families play in developing their children's psychological wellbeing. I want to thank my parents Anne and Jerry, for laying the foundations of my mental fitness. Thank you to my father whose endless optimism never ceased to amaze me and to my mother whose willingness to allow me to fail, as well as her empathy, gratitude and kindness resonate deeply with me. I would also like to thank my brother Mark who allowed me to go on this parenting journey with him. A special thank you goes to Mitchell who brings joy to my life every day and willingly allowed me to share our story.

Thank you to my husband and number one fan, Andrew, for his unwavering support and belief that I can accomplish whatever I set out to do. I could not imagine life without you, my best friend and lighthouse keeper.

I want to finally thank every parent and educator who reads this book and takes the time to help children embed these positive habits of mind so they become second nature to them, just like putting on sunscreen. That is how we raise a mentally fit generation.

References

Why adults are understandably worried

Goleman, D. (2006). *Social Intelligence: The New Science of Human Relationships*. Bantam Dell.

The Mental Health of Children and Adolescents (2015). Report of the Second Australian Child and Adolescent Survey of Mental Health and Wellbeing. Retrieved from https://www1.health.gov.au/internet/main/publishing.nsf/Content/9DA8CA21306FE6EDC A257E2700016945/$File/child2.pdf

The Royal Children's Hospital Melbourne Child Health Poll (2017). Retrieved from https://www.rchpoll.org.au/polls/child-mental-health-problemscan-parents-spot-the-signs/

United Kingdom Children's Commissioner Report (2017). Retrieved from https://www.childrenscommissioner.gov.uk/2017/07/04/shocking-report-by-childrens-commissioner-reveals-millions-of-children-in-england-living-vulnerable-or-high-risk-lives/

World Health Organisation Report on Child and Adolescent Mental Health (2017). Retrieved from https://www.who.int/mental_health/maternal-child/child_adolescent/en/ https://www.who.int/mental_health/evidence/atlas/profiles-2017/en/

The protective nature of mental fitness

Robinson, P. (2016). *Practising Positive Education: A Guide to Improve Wellbeing Literacy in Schools*. Positive Psychology Institute, Pty. Ltd.

World Health Organization. (2009); *World Health Organization Report on Global Health Risks: Mortality and Burden of Disease Attributable to Selected Major Risks* Retrieved from https://www.who.int/healthinfo/global_burden_disease/GlobalHealthRisks_report_full.pdf

The building blocks of mental fitness

Neal, D. T., Wood, W., & Quinn, J. M. (2006). Habits – A Repeat Performance. *Current Directions in Psychological Science*, 15(4),198–202.

Zero to Three (2016). *Tuning In: Parents of Young Children Tell Us What They Think, Know and Need National Parent Survey Outcomes* Retrieved from https://www.zerotothree.org/resources/1424-national-parent-survey-overview-and-key-insights

Teaching brain basics

Jacka, F., O'Neil, A., Quirk, S.E., Housden, S., Brennan, S.L., Williams, L.J., Pasco, J.A., & Berk, M. (2014). The relationship between diet and mental health in children and adolescents: A systematic review. *American Journal of Public Health*, 104(10), 31–42.

Siegel, D., & Bryson, T. (2011). *The Whole-Brain Child: Revolutionary Strategies to Nurture Your Child's Developing Mind*. Scribe Publications.

Stickgold, R. (2017). Interview with PBS – Why humans have to snooze. Retrieved from https://www.pbs.org/newshour/extra/daily-videos/why-humans-have-to-snooze/

Cultivating optimism

Seligman, M. E. P., Reivich, K., Jaycox, L., & Gillham, J. (1996). *The Optimistic Child: Proven Program to Safeguard Children from Depression & Build Lifelong Resilience*. Houghton Mifflin.

Seligman, M. E. P. (2006). *Learned Optimism: How to Change Your Mind and Your Life*. Vintage Books.

Managing emotions

Fredrickson, B.L. (2009). *Positivity*. Three Rivers Press.

Goleman, D. (1995). *Emotional Intelligence: Why it can Matter More than IQ*. Bantam Books.

Gottman, J., & Declaire, J. (1997). *Raising an Emotionally Intelligent Child*. Simon & Schuster.

Jones, D.E., Greenberg, M., & Crowley, M. (2015). Early Social-Emotional Functioning and Public Health: The Relationship Between Kindergarten Social Competence and Future Wellness. *American Journal of Public Health*, 105(11), 2283–2290.

Siegel, D., & Bryson, T. (2011). *The Whole-Brain Child: Revolutionary Strategies to Nurture Your Child's Developing Mind*. Scribe Publications.

Yale Centre for Emotional Intelligence (2019). Retrieved from http://ei.yale.edu/

Recognising their strengths

Linley, A. (2008). *Average to A+: Realising Strengths in Yourself and Others*. CAPP Press.

Peterson, C., & Seligman, M.E.P. (2004). *Character Strengths and Virtues: A Handbook and Classification*. Oxford University Press.

Waters, L. (2017). *The Strength Switch: How the New Science of Strength Based Parenting Helps Your Child and Teen to Flourish*. Penguin.

Waters, L. (2019). Visible Wellbeing Program. Retrieved from http://www.visiblewellbeing.org/

Making friends

Anthony, M., & Lindert, R. (2010). *Little Girls Can Be Mean: Four steps to bully-proof girls in the early grades.* Griffin.

Australian Government Anti-Bullying website: *Bullying No Way* Retrieved from https://bullyingnoway.gov.au/WhatIsBullying/ DefinitionOfBullying

Baxter, J. (2020). *University of Queensland Global Prevalence of Bullying Survey 2020.* Retrieved from https://www.uq.edu.au/ news/article/2020/02/global-study-finds-almost-one-third-of-school-students-bullied

Ortiz-Ospina, E. (2019). *Is there a loneliness epidemic?* Retrieved from https://ourworldindata.org/loneliness-epidemic

Waldinger, R. (2019). *Harvard Study of Adult Development* Retrieved from https://www.adultdevelopmentstudy.org/

Encouraging kindness and empathy

Brown, B. (2017). *Braving the Wilderness: The Quest for True Belonging and the Courage to Stand Alone.* Random House.

Korb, A. (2015). *The Upward Spiral: Using Neuroscience to Reverse the Course of Depression, One Small Change at a Time.* New Harbinger Publications.

Korb, A. Published articles and thesis Retrieved from https:// alexkorbphd.com/

Lieberman, M. (2013) *Social: Why Our Brains are Wired to Connect.* Crown Publishing Group.

Fostering gratitude

Emmons, R. A., & McCullough, M. E. (2004). *The Psychology of Gratitude.* Oxford University Press.

Learning to fail

Big Life Journal resources Retrieved from https://biglifejournal.com/

Duckworth, A. L., Peterson, C., Matthews, M. D., & Kelly, D. R. (2007). Grit: Perseverance and Passion for Long-Term Goals. *Journal of Personality and Social Psychology*, 92(6), 1087–1101.

Dweck, C. S. (2006). *Mindset: The New Psychology of Success.* Random House Publishing.

Yeager, D. S., Johnson, R., Spitzer, B. J., Trzesniewski, K. H., Powers, J., & Dweck, C. S. (2014). The far-reaching effects of believing people can change: Implicit theories of personality shape stress, health, and achievement during adolescence. *Journal of Personality and Social Psychology*, 106(6), 867–884.

Self-mastery

Taylor, J. (2011). *Your Children are Listening: Nine Messages They Need to Hear from You.* The Experiment.

Practising mindfulness

Clarke-Fields, H. (2019). *Raising Good Humans: A Mindful Guide to Breaking the Cycle of Reactive Parenting and Raising Kind Confident Kids.* New Harbinger Publications Inc..

Hooker, K.E., & Fodor, I.E. (2008). Teaching Mindfulness to Children. *Gestalt Review*, 12 (1), 75–91.

Wardle, J., & Weinhardt, M. (2013). *The Everything Parents Guide to Raising Mindful Children: Giving Parents the Tools to Teach Emotional Awareness, Coping Skills and Impulse Control in Children.* Everything Publishing House.

Lightning Source UK Ltd.
Milton Keynes UK
UKHW020704270223
417728UK00015B/1249